Succeeding in School and Beyond

Succeeding in School and Beyond

The Elements of Achievement

Fred Hageman

New Avenue Press
Oakland, California

www.achievementelements.com

New Avenue Press
2710 E. 22nd Street
Oakland, CA 94601

Succeeding in School and Beyond: The Elements of Achievement is a completely revised edition of *Making the Grades: How You Can Achieve Greater Success With Less Stress in School and Beyond.* ©1995 by Frederick Hageman.

Quotes by Paramahansa Yogananda from *Where There is Light: Insight and Inspiration for Meeting Life's Challenges* (Self-Realization Fellowship, Los Angeles, CA) Used by permission.

Cataloging in Publication Data
Hageman, Fred.
Succeeding in school and beyond: the elements of achievement
/ Fred Hageman.

1. Success–Juvenile literature. 2. Study, Method of–
Juvenile literature. 3. Study skills I. Title
BJ1611.H34 1995   94-68681
371.3028–dc21

ISBN 0-9764601-8-1

Disclaimer

Printed in the United States of America.

Inspiration without instruction is in vain.
To declare there is a mountaintop of promise is useless or worse,
if I am left in the valley of doubt.
It is one thing to tell me I have greatness within,
yet another to teach me how to bring it out.
Do not tell me I should fly if you cannot show me how.

Contents

To accomplish great things, we must not only act,
but also dream, not only plan, but also believe.
—Anatole France

Always bear in mind that your own resolution to succeed
is more important than any other one thing.
—Abraham Lincoln

Never underestimate the power of dreams
and the influence of the human spirit.
We are all the same in this notion.
The potential for greatness lives within each of us.
—Wilma Rudolph

We were born to succeed, not to fail.
—Henry David Thoreau

Introduction

Kids do not become good learners; they become poor learners.
Children start off naturally loving and excelling at learning—
it's what they do all day long.
Then, far too often, something gets in the way
and the struggle begins.

W hen it comes to what's wrong with the schools, there is no shortage of opinion, much of it conflicting. But one thing virtually everyone agrees on is that student readiness makes all the difference in the world when it comes to how well someone is going to do in school. In the same school situation, the student who is willing to work and ready to learn has a far greater chance of succeeding than the one who is not.

Obviously, it is important to do everything possible to improve the schools, but while you are waiting and waiting and waiting for that to happen, here's something that can help you right now. This is not a book about fixing the schools or what the schools should do. It isn't about schools at all. It's about the *elements of achievement*. These six elements—identity, belief, visualization, goals, focus, and state of mind—make up the mental framework you, me, and everyone else works from when we set out to accomplish anything.

1

This is *not* a book about study skills. There are plenty of study guides available, so why write another one? Unlike these other methods, however, *Succeeding in School and Beyond* deals with the underlying obstacles that can stop someone from reaching their potential. If you are a student, the material here can help you improve your performance, both in school and in anything else you are interested in. It is not difficult to learn. If you are a parent or teacher wanting to help your kids succeed, the material here is not difficult to teach.

Because the elements work in the same way regardless of where you apply them, you can also learn them using any pursuit you want. This makes a huge difference, especially if you've been having difficulty in school. It's not hard to understand why you might not be excited about learning the typical study guide stuff. Even though study skills are important, let's face it: not only are they connected with school, the very thing you've been having difficulty with, but they're also pretty boring. That's not a very compelling combination, is it?

One of the best things about the elements of achievement is that you can learn how to use them by applying them to something you already enjoy or are interested in learning. In fact, when teaching this stuff, I don't start with anything connected with school. Instead, I use what the person is interested in and tailor the material to that. I've worked with people improving their abilities in things like doing bike tricks, batting average, foul-shooting, guitar playing, dieting, wrestling—even video games. As long as it is something that can be measured and turned into a goal, it can be used to show how the achievement process works.

Once you see how it all works, you can then apply it to your academic situation. And once you begin to see that much greater success *is* possible, you might just become a lot more open to learning useful things like study skills and other aids because your motivation will be greater than before.

Another important feature about the material here is that it isn't necessary to learn everything about it before using it. Because each of the elements affects the others, once you grab on to any of them, the rest tend to come along for the ride. This is one of the best things about knowing how to use this stuff, and a critical point for parents or teachers teaching this to their kids.

Once you jump onboard, turnarounds can be dramatic, which fuels your motivation. Also, unlike some school subjects and the study skills approaches, the elements of achievement are not left behind once you finish school. This gives you a tremendous jump on the future. Once they become a conscious part of your day-to-day experience, they naturally carry over into any career or personal goals you might want to accomplish.

I know of no more encouraging fact than the unquestionable ability of man to elevate his life by conscious endeavor.
—*Henry David Thoreau*

When people talk about the problems in the schools, you will often hear statements such as, "it is every student's right to receive a quality education." As good as this sounds, it's putting things exactly the wrong way around because rights have nothing to do with it. Certainly, it is everyone's right to have a quality education provided, but that is another issue entirely. As a student, why might you be having difficulty receiving what the teachers are delivering in the first place?

It's a lot like in football. The quarterback's job is to deliver the ball, but that's all that he can do. In order for the play to be successful, it's up to the receiver to catch the ball, isn't it? It doesn't matter how good the blocking is, how well executed the offensive scheme, or how fine the throw—if the receiver drops the ball, no touchdown. It's the same in school. It makes no difference how well planned the lesson is, or how varied, if the student drops the ball. In order for education to be successful, it has to be *received*. Regardless of how often it is overlooked, this is not a minor point, and it goes straight back to student readiness.

You know the old saying about something going in one ear and out the other? Often, the truth is more like something goes in one ear, hits something hard, and bounces out. That "something hard" is a mental barrier consisting of difficulties such as disempowering beliefs ("I can't get good grades," "I hate school," "I'm just not good at taking tests," "It's boring," etc.), failing to set and follow clear-cut goals, poor focus, habitually negative states, and fear of failure.

It's this kind of junk that blocks potential. Can you imagine a successful person in any field laboring under such a habitual mental environment? If *you* are dealing with this type of garbage, is it any wonder you might be having difficulty? The good news is that even if you are, the situation is definitely fixable. *Succeeding in School and Beyond* is about helping you remove the barriers that get in the way of success and learning how to align the elements of achievement. For example:

✦What if someone who hated school because she was convinced she was a failure could learn how to consistently believe in herself and her ability to succeed?

✦What if someone who had no direction could learn how to create clearly defined goals and plans for achieving them?

✦What if someone who always saw the worst in whatever situation could learn instead to focus on what was valuable in the same situation and use it to his advantage?

✦What if someone who was so afraid of failure that she crippled her chances of succeeding could learn how to work through that fear and perform successfully?

✦What if someone could learn how to do well in subjects he disliked?

✦What if someone who had little motivation because of previous failures could learn how to get beyond that failure and experience positive results?

For many of us, the idea of changing in order to succeed in a greater way can be a frightening prospect, especially if we doubt our present abilities to make or sustain these changes. Often, however, great results don't require great changes nearly as much as they require small, simple changes consistently applied. Instead of having to expend a great deal more time or effort, it's more often a matter of changing direction or becoming aware of something that was slowing down your progress without your realizing it. When you see how the elements of achievement work together, you will see that this is indeed the case.

As an illustration, suppose your goal is to shoot an arrow as far as possible. What do you have to do? Take the bow, place the arrow, pull back the bowstring as far as you can and let the arrow fly. That's all there is to it, right? But what's the difference between shooting an arrow high and far and shooting an arrow into the ground? It's the same amount of time and effort involved, but the direction you aim makes all the difference, doesn't it?

The techniques and strategies in this book are simple. This being the case, some people have difficulty believing that they can lead to such an increase in successful results. A lot of times the hardest thing is letting go of preconceptions. The second hardest thing seems to be getting over the, "yeah, yeah, I know, but . . ." syndrome. As I've said, none of the stuff here is that hard to learn, but don't let the simplicity fool you. There's power in it that you will miss out on if you just assume it's too simple.

> *Great things are not done by impulse,*
> *but by a series of small things brought together.*
> —*Vincent Van Gogh*

Here's an example of what I mean. Throughout his NBA career, Charles Barkley was among the leaders in rebounds, even though he was a lot shorter than the players he was going up against night after night. When asked about what techniques he relied upon for his success, he said, "I always laugh when people ask me about rebounding techniques. I've got a technique. It's called 'just go get the damn ball.'"

What could be simpler than that? But when you unpack it, there is a wealth of information in that simple statement. What he is saying is that too often players get so caught up in having the proper technique that they lose sight of the main objective: getting the ball. It was this laser beam focus along with unwavering determination and dedication to achieving his goal that allowed Sir Charles to consistently succeed against much taller competition. It's a very simple point, but one that many players ignore or overlook. Don't let the simplicity of the material here fool you. Just go get the ball.

We all work with the elements of achievement regardless of the results we get. If you use them in a haphazard or negative way, you generally produce negative results. If you use them in a deliberate, positive manner, you generally get positive results. Unlike skills that are specific to certain fields, the elements cross over into all fields. This is why you find people from diverse times and backgrounds saying similar things when it comes to the elements of achievement, as the many quotes demonstrate.

We are what we repeatedly do.
Excellence then, is not an act, but a habit.
—Aristotle

So please realize that in learning about the elements, it is most definitely *not* a matter of acquiring new skills, but about becoming aware of what you are already doing and taking conscious control of it. I may be bringing something to your attention or showing you how something works, but don't forget for a second that the elements are factory-installed equipment. It's never a matter of *not* using the elements, because that just isn't possible. We all use them all day every day. The key is in *how* we use them, in which direction we aim them. So let's take a look:

✦*Identity:* Our identity is the sum of the beliefs we have about ourselves. How we habitually *see ourselves* determines our performance level, our ability to tap inner resources, what attitudes we have, how hard we will work, and what results we expect. People who are consistently succeeding have developed identities that lead them to expect successful results because that is *who they are.*

✦*Belief:* Beliefs drive our behavior. We do not produce results based on our abilities, but on what we believe our abilities to be. Too often, we allow limiting beliefs to constrict our performance, convincing ourselves that we cannot achieve something. People who are consistently succeeding perform based on the belief that they *can* do what they set out to do.

✦*Visualization:* Visualizing is seeing results in advance. Our minds respond to strongly imagined ideas *as if* they are real and guide our behavior accordingly. All too often, we expect to fail in most situations, and spend much time and energy visualizing negative results. People who are consistently succeeding spend most of their mental effort visualizing successful results. Performance then follows in turn.

✦*Goals:* Setting goals is essential to success. Without goals, any problem that comes along affects us greatly because, without the long-range vision provided by goals, the problem is all that we can see. By locking onto our goal, we can move beyond the obstacles. Goals provide motivation, momentum, and direction. People who are consistently succeeding understand the power of goals and know how to set them.

✦*Focus:* Our conscious minds cannot take in everything happening around us or within us, so we focus on only a narrow portion of sensory and mental stimuli. When we work from a negative focus, we look for what is wrong in a situation and we *will* find it. People who are consistently succeeding have learned how to look for what is valuable or useful in a situation, and also how to keep their focus trained on what they want to accomplish and their plan for achieving it.

✦*State of Mind:* Our state governs how we perceive a given situation as well as how we react to it. We all have within us great resources to aid us in achieving our goals. But when burdened by habitually negative states, we fail to tap these resources. People who are consistently succeeding use a far greater percentage of their resources because they have learned to work from constructive states.

There's nothing complicated about these elements, is there? But imagine them aligned and working together. With a little practice, you can use them in a positive way and achieve much more—even if you've been doing poorly up to this point.

Of course, working with the elements of achievement isn't going to replace the acquisition of basic skills and subject knowledge that you need to be successful in your studies. Please understand that I am not suggesting this in the least. Instead, think of aligning the elements as a high-octane gasoline additive. An engine cannot run on an additive alone, but its performance will be greatly enhanced when the additive is used. It's the same way with the elements and subject knowledge.

When it comes to consistently being able to achieve, whether we are talking about long-term or short-term goals, the whole procedure can be boiled down to its essence, what I call the *achievement process:* Know exactly what you are going for, consistently see yourself as having already accomplished it, fully expect that you will do so, and feel that way.

A common response upon first hearing this process is "you have *got* to be kidding. It can't be *that* simple!" But I'm not kidding, and yes, it really *is* that simple. If you consistently work the achievement process, your elements will be properly aligned. This is the key to succeeding, regardless of the pursuit.

But getting to that point of alignment (or staying there) can be difficult. The problems come in when the negative aspects of the elements stop you from consistently following through. When you are battling yourself because of this negativity, you restrict your potential and cut down on your chances of succeeding. It's kind of like punching holes in your own boat. By the time you finish this book, however, you will have a far better understanding of the power in the achievement process, as well as some effective ways of dealing with the junk that gets in the way of your using it.

Succeeding in School and Beyond is not about tricks or gimmicks. There isn't any hocus-pocus magic wand here, no hype, nor any false claims. It's about teaching you how to significantly improve the odds for success in both your schoolwork and whatever else you are interested in. If you apply the concepts here, you will be able to access far more of the resources and abilities you already have within you, even if you don't currently believe you have them because of past failures.

Give yourself a chance by giving this a chance. The strategies and techniques included here are as old as the hills and have been thoroughly tested by people from all walks of life all throughout history. There isn't anything that I just made up. In a nutshell, if you work the elements, they work for you. But without the spark from you—the desire to take this stuff and run with it—this is all just a bunch of words. Add that spark, however, and there is power here to burn.

Education is not filling a bucket, but lighting a fire.
—*William Butler Yeats*

One's mind, once stretched by a new idea,
never regains its original dimensions.
—*Oliver Wendell Holmes*

Chapter One

Identity—
Who Are You, Anyway?

Self-image sets the boundaries of individual accomplishment.
—Maxwell Maltz

We cannot rise higher than our thought of ourselves.
—Orison Swett Marden

Imagine a school. Let's call it School A. The facilities at School A are first-rate. The buildings are clean and well lit, heated and air-conditioned according to season. The classrooms are carpeted, the windows open wide and close tight, and the desks are new, with all four legs flush on the floor.

The book room is packed with clean textbooks, complete with covers and all of the pages intact. The library has a wide variety of books, and there are computerized catalogs for easy access. The computer room, photo lab, ceramics room, auto shop and band room are well equipped and well maintained, and the school newspaper is put out every Friday. For assemblies, the auditorium can seat the entire student body. The gymnasium and athletic fields are spacious, with new bleachers, and the cafeteria serves healthy food that kids actually like.

If that sounds like a dream, let's consider a nightmare. Imagine another school, School B. The facilities at School B can't quite compare to those at School A. Everyone agrees it looks like a prison. The rooms are small and poorly ventilated (unless you count broken windows.) Many of the ancient desks are broken and the blackboards are in need of repair. The book room doesn't have enough books for the students, who must either share or buy their own, but the ones it does have sometimes have covers. The library doesn't have a large number of books either, and most of them are older than the kids. The one computer in the school is in the attendance office, but it doesn't work that well or that often. Tales of actual labs and shops are sometimes heard, but these facilities are generally regarded to have disappeared back when students stopped walking uphill both ways in the July snow. There is no school newspaper because of a lack of equipment and interest. There is no auditorium, so if there is an assembly, it must be held twice so that all of the students can be seated on the remaining unbroken bleachers in the gym. The cafeteria serves something like food, but there is a stigma attached to eating it, since anyone who has an alternative to doing so acts upon it.

Two Students

Now consider two students. Student A comes to class every day, on time, with paper, pen or pencil, and the required textbook and assignment. Attentive when the teacher is speaking, she participates readily, offering thoughtful comments and questions. When an assignment is given, she doesn't complain, but makes sure she understands the directions and writes them, as well as the due date, in her notebook. She is well liked and is sought out regularly for help, which she gives freely and cheerfully. During study period, or if she has any free time during a class, she begins her homework and finishes it promptly when she gets home. People joke that she doesn't even have to try to maintain her straight A's, but no one really believes it. Although she is constantly busy, she always seems full of energy. No one has ever heard her complain about being tired or stressed out, but she *was* overheard quietly expressing concern over which university was offering her the best scholarship.

Student B, on the other hand, comes to class three or four days a week, but is often both late and unprepared. Interrupting the teacher when she arrives, she holds up class in order to tell why she was late and find someone who will give her paper and a pen. Frequently talking to both those students next to her and those across the room, she apologizes when told to be quiet and actually is for almost a minute. During discussions, she often disparages other students' comments, makes jokes, or asks, "What time do we get out of here?"

When an assignment is given, she automatically complains that it is boring and/or stupid, and tells how another teacher has already given an assignment. She makes sure to add that she has to go to work that night and that she doesn't have time for all of this stupid busywork. Once she grudgingly accepts the fact that she has to do the boring and/or stupid assignment, she then lobbies to get the due date pushed back. When this fails, she asks that the assignment be repeated, but doesn't write it down because her notebook is in her locker, and besides, she can always get it from another student.

She is always asking for help, but what she really wants is the answers, or someone to copy the assignment from. During study periods, she socializes and maintains that she doesn't have any homework or has several reasons why she can't work on it in class and will do it at home. Upon getting her assignments back, she inevitably argues that she should have received a higher grade and gets mad at the teacher, claiming she is being picked on. She often falls asleep in class because a) she is tired, b) she doesn't feel well, c) the teacher is boring, d) all of the above. She frequently tells anyone who will listen that school sucks and has nothing to do with the "real world," which, come to think of it, she doesn't think is all that great either. Generally, the rest of the class feels better when she is not there.

Some cause happiness wherever they go; others, whenever they go.
—Oscar Wilde

School Quality Doesn't Determine Student Success Nearly as Much as Identity Does

Certainly, everyone is concerned with the quality of their school and would prefer that it was more like School A. However, the truth is that it is not the quality of the school that primarily determines how a student will do academically. Of course, I am not saying that school conditions and teacher quality are unimportant, for they surely are. But there are always kids like Student B in School A, and there are always kids like Student A in School B. Will the benefits and advantages of School A make a difference if a student is just sitting there, staring out the window? Similarly, will the disadvantages of School B stop a student from succeeding if that student has the determination and drive to do so? In both instances, the answer is no. In both cases, student readiness is going to determine performance level far more than the teacher or the conditions in the school.

One of the most important factors in determining how a student performs is identity. Before just about anything else, it is how you *see yourself* that will determine the level you perform at on a consistent basis. Now, before you reject this out of hand, think about it. Who gets A's? You could say that the smart kids do, but there are many smart kids that don't get A's. Is hard work the trick? Again, many kids who work quite hard don't get A's. The same applies to those who "kiss up." In fact, there's only one type of student who consistently gets A's, and that is an A student. Although this seems painfully obvious, it is critically important that you understand the point here. What is it about students who get A's consistently and those who do not? As I've said, and as you know from your own classes, it is not always the smartest students or the hardest working students who get the best grades. The students who get A's are the students who expect to get A's.

> *What a man thinks of himself,*
> *that is what determines, or rather indicates, his fate.*
> —*Henry David Thoreau*

Expectation is the Key to Student Identity
Notice that they don't want, or merely think they deserve A's, but they *expect* to get A's. The difference between merely wanting something and expecting to get something is enormous, and

it is this expectation that sets those students who get A's apart from the rest. It's not a matter of being conceited or thinking they are better than anyone else, either. They simply know that they are going to do the necessary work, with the necessary attitude, to get the job done.

If you want to be an A student, the first and most important step for you to take is to work on becoming an A student in identity. When you become an A student in identity, it will be easier for you to get A's than to not get A's. If you don't make being an A student part of your identity, you will find that you probably will not reach your goal consistently, even if you are working harder.

You did take note of the part about doing the necessary work, didn't you? We're not talking hocus-pocus magic wand here. We're talking about getting the most out of the abilities you already have by learning to do the things that bring them to the surface and breaking down the barriers that stop them from doing so. Identity is a vital part of this process. Think of professional athletes. How is it that they can continually perform at such high levels with all of that pressure and scrutiny when most people would crumble under similar circumstances? A former major-league baseball manager hit on a key factor: "Professional athletes are inherently competitive. They wouldn't make it to the top level unless they wanted and expected to complete every pass, bat 1.000, or score a goal in every game."

I'm not out there just to be dancing around.
I expect to win every time I tee up.
—*Lee Trevino*

Hey, I Take Exception to That Statement

But wait a minute. Isn't it true that we often hear of people who have accomplished something saying afterwards that they didn't expect to be that successful? Does this mean that what I am saying here is nonsense? Before jumping to that conclusion, consider another question: Do you think these people actively expected to fail and put their efforts into doing so?

The old saying about there being an exception to every rule is true, but you don't want to let yourself get caught up in a search and destroy mission because of this fact. Hey, I'm sure that if you look hard enough, you can find an exception to virtually everything I am talking about in this book. I certainly know that I can. So what? That doesn't mean that the stuff here is false, just that there are going to be exceptions. There always are. That's just the way it is.

An exception is only an instance that does not conform to a rule or generalization. Dismissing something because of an exception is nothing more than attempting to turn an exception into a rule. So for the principle of expectation as well as for everything else we are examining, there are going to be exceptions. That's perfectly ok, and brings us to another old saying: The exception proves the rule. This means that if it were not for the rule, you wouldn't be able to recognize the exception.

For example, Albert Einstein was a poor student when he was in school. He was working as a clerk in a patent office, doing physics in his spare time when he developed his groundbreaking theory of relativity and that most famous of all equations, $E=mc^2$. Now, if you were interested in becoming a physicist, do you think the smartest way to pursue your dream would be to be a poor student, seek work in a patent office, and do physics in your spare time because that's what Einstein did?

So please keep in mind that what we are dealing with here are general principles that have proven themselves over and over for people from every background imaginable. There will always be exceptions, certainly, but as far as averages go, these are the principles that have been demonstrated to produce consistent success time and time again. And one of the principles is that the people who succeed most consistently are those who expect to do so.

> *High achievement always takes place*
> *in the framework of high expectation.*
> —*Charles Kettering*

Who Are You?

Identity is a key for anyone who produces consistent results. Unfortunately, it doesn't just work for producing positive results. Don't you know someone who, regardless of what he or she sets out to do, winds up reverting back to the same old person they were before they started? What happens too often in these situations is that the person tried to make changes outwardly, but failed to make the necessary changes in identity that would allow those changes to stick. Therefore, on some level they didn't expect the changes to stick. Identity is one of the most important factors in changing the way you are behaving. If you want to have lasting change, you must first change the way you perceive yourself in that particular area. If you want to see real examples of what I am talking about, just look at all the kids who swear at the beginning of each report period that *this* time they are going to get better grades, pay attention, work harder, blah, blah, blah. And they mean it, they really do. At least for a few days. Then, all the old identity elements resurface and it's business as usual.

> *They are able because they think they are able.*
> —*Virgil*

What is identity? The simplest way to understand it is to begin with a question: Who are you? The easiest answer would be, "I'm Joe or Jenny So and so." But does this answer capture who you really are? Obviously, it doesn't, because there is much more to a person's identity than their name. Your identity is the sum of the beliefs you have about yourself that make you different from everyone else. It is what makes you, *you*. With a little thought, you will realize that there are many facets, or sides, to your identity.

Take a look at the different ways in which you perceive yourself. Perhaps you see yourself as an athlete or a musician, as an actor or an artist. Maybe you see yourself as someone who is intense or funny, someone who is accepted or misunderstood, someone who is basically happy, or generally sad. Do you see yourself as a winner? A loser? "I'm too thin." "I'm too fat." "I'm awkward." "I'm really good looking." "I'm ugly." "I've got it made." "I'll never get it right."

These are some of the ways in which people see themselves, and it is fair to say that these labels never quite tell the whole story. As I said, we are all multifaceted people. The important thing to remember is that, along with the other aspects of your identity, you are sure to add in the fact that you are also a successful student. The elements you are learning here are the ingredients for doing just this.

We Perform According to the Guidelines of Our Identity

What is it about identity that makes it so important? In a significant sense, our minds are a lot like computers. The results that we get out of them depend greatly upon the software (expectations and beliefs) that we put into them. The old computer saying, "garbage in, garbage out" applies equally well to our minds because it is our minds, in accordance with our identity, that will determine how much of our resources we will use, how hard we will work, what attitude we have, and what results we will expect. That's a lot of action riding on how you see yourself, so take a look at what's going on with it.

Did you ever notice that those people who are always talking about how they never can do this or that, how this or that is going to go wrong, or why this or that won't work out usually wind up being right? This is because your mind will guide your experience along the lines of the way you see things. It will run the program that you load into it. If you've loaded an identity program that tells your mind that you are the kind of person who consistently does what is needed to get the job done, what kind of results do you think you will get? You will get results that are in accordance with that identity.

This isn't just a matter of psyching yourself up, although that is also an important factor. What happens when you adopt an identity is that you start perceiving yourself as someone who behaves in a certain way. Since that is "who you are," your ability to tap inner resources is shaped accordingly, as is how hard you will work, what attitude you will have, and what results you will expect. And, yes, this goes both ways. If you are laboring under an identity program which says you just don't come up with the goods because you aren't that kind of person, well, guess what?

This is the role identity plays in the achievement process: Know exactly what you are going for, consistently see yourself as having already accomplished it, **fully expect that you will do so**, and feel that way.

I never intended to become a run-of-the-mill person.
—*Barbara Jordan*

You Don't Have to "Earn" Your Identity Before Using It
A lot of people believe that in order to change their identity they must first produce the results so that they are "permitted" to have the identity that goes along with those results. Initial objections run along the lines of, "How can I just change who I am? Wouldn't I be lying if I pretended to be someone I'm really not? Wouldn't I be a hypocrite?" You don't want to fall into this type of thinking because it only hampers your progress. If you do think in this way, you will have to fight against the identity of being someone who doesn't "deserve" successful results yet. Besides, this idea isn't as strange as it might sound at first. When kids are out playing on the street, court, or field, how often are they pretending to be their favorite athlete? People are always imitating those they respect. This is the whole point about role models—acting *as if*—and it's a natural thing to do.

If there are specific results you want, you've got to begin by seeing yourself as the type of person who already gets those kinds of results. When you do, things will begin falling in line with the way you see yourself. This idea of seeing things *as if* they already are that way is going to keep coming up. It's one of the most important keys to the whole deal, so let it sink in deep.

> *If you want a quality, act as if you already have it.*
> —William James

But let's be clear about what is going on here. You are not going to be a hypocrite or a liar *if* you are sincere in your intention to become the kind of person who gets the results you are after. Of course, it should be pointed out that you don't have to go around announcing your new identity to everyone. Your new results will speak for themselves and *they* will announce your new identity for you.

Of course, if you really are just trying to fake your way through something for short-term gain, you will not only be a hypocrite, but you will most likely fail as well. This is not, I trust, the combination you want to pursue. There is the well-known idea of "fake it until you make it," but it is based on a sincere effort to become something, not a fraudulent attempt to pull one over on someone. Although it is easy to lie to other people, you can't deceive your mind, at least not for long. If, on one hand, you meekly tell yourself, "I am an A student," but on the other hand, you are constantly undercutting this message by telling yourself, "Well, ok, not *really*," your mind will listen to the dominant program and guide you in that direction.

We All Want to Be Right

Identity is critical because of our inherent interest in being correct. Everybody wants to be right, right? This is because it's obviously a lot more fun than being wrong. Did you ever know someone who insisted they were right even when all of the evidence was clearly against them? "Don't confuse me with facts." Or, did you ever know anyone who twisted the facts in order to appear right, someone who, no matter what angle you approach them from, they turn it toward their argument?

For example, say Jenny complains to Joe: "You're always too busy. You never spend any time with me!" He insists that he does. She continues on, saying, "No, you never spend any time with me!" He then lists several instances recently where they did something together. "But you never do what I want to do!" "Sure I do," he says, and then names several instances where he did what she had wanted to do. "Yeah, but you didn't *really* want to." On and on it goes.

Hey, we all like to be correct. This is why identity is so important. If you are working from a disempowering identity, one that looks for what can go wrong, one that "knows" it can't be done, your mind is going to interpret events and evidence to accommodate your identity's need to be right. Similarly, if you are working from an empowering identity, one that looks for what is beneficial, one that "knows" that something *can* be done, your mind is going to accommodate your identity by interpreting events and evidence accordingly. We all want to be right.

So which kind of identity do you want to cultivate? Do you want to spend your time trying to prove to yourself and to others that you are "right" when you insist that you just can't do something? Do you want to prove to people that you can't really be expected to produce *those* kinds of results because *you* aren't that type of person? Or do you want to get positive results because you want to prove to yourself and to others that you *are* that type of person?

Whatever direction you move in, you are going to be working to prove something in order to be correct. Which way you go is up to you.

Why Should Changing Your Identity Be So Strange?

Of course, some people are bound to think that the idea of changing their identity is a bit weird, but it really isn't. You *can* change your identity. You've been doing it all your life. In fact, if you didn't do it, you wouldn't be walking, or talking, or riding a bike, or reading, or writing, or any of the things that you've learned to do that have changed the way you perceive yourself.

If you still doubt that you can change your identity, ask yourself a question: Where did you get the identity you've got now? Did it come intact, perhaps with a wave of a magic wand? Take a closer look. It came in small installments, piece by piece.

Here's how it works: Take a particular incident like forgetting an assignment, or your backpack, or whatever. You realize what you've done and say to yourself, "I forgot it." Ok, this is not a big deal. But if you wind up forgetting something else soon after, you may begin telling yourself that you are a forgetful person. With the repetition of a few acts of forgetfulness, you begin running an "I'm just so forgetful" program in your mind. Soon, every time you forget something, you say, "See, I'm forgetful."

Hey, you've just created a piece of your identity. So you have to be careful that you don't acquire disempowering beliefs by turning one or two actions into disempowering notions of "the way you are." There's a big difference between "I forgot" and "I'm forgetful," between "I did poorly on that test" and "I just can't take tests." Perhaps the biggest reason why so many people are terrible when it comes to remembering names is because they reinforce the idea every time they forget someone's name by telling the other person *and themselves* how horrible they are with names.

When we start to investigate our identity, we begin to see that we are influenced by many factors, including family, friends, TV and movies. This is only natural. Whatever the influences, you need to keep in mind that your identity is constantly shifting according to the dominant beliefs that you hold. Since it *is* going to change, you want to control the direction it moves in, instead of having it shift and then just accepting the changes as "the way it is" and falling in line with them because, "that's the just the way I am."

> *First say to yourself what you would be;*
> *and then do what you have to do.*
> —*Epictetus*

Who Do You Want to Be?

Think of all of the ways to fill in the question: "Who am I?" Write down as many elements of your identity as you can think of, whether they come from physical traits, mental traits, emotional traits, achievements, etc. Don't worry about whether they are good or bad, or right or wrong, or anything like that. Just write down as much as you can think of.

Now think of all the things you would like to accomplish. Without thinking about whether you could actually be that way or not, make a list of the characteristics you would need to have in order to accomplish these things and write them down. How would you need to be?

Before you can do something, you must first be something.
—*Johann Wolfgang Goethe*

Look at each list. Are there any characteristics that are on both? These are strong elements to use for the foundation of your identity because you already have them programmed into your mind. The other elements on your second list are the parts of your new identity you will be working to acquire as we proceed. Please don't worry if you don't think you can become such a person. The truth is that at this moment, you really don't know the extent of what you can or can't do.

If we all did the things we are capable of doing,
we would literally astound ourselves.
—*Thomas Edison*

Just focus on what you want, and how you would need to be in order to succeed. As for the elements of your present identity that you don't like, just leave them aside at this time. After learning to program more empowering beliefs into your mind's computer, you will see that many of these old characteristics will start to fall away because, having so much evidence to the contrary, you aren't going to believe in them anymore.

So now that you understand that changing your identity is the key to changing the results you get on a consistent basis, we need to examine the building blocks of both your identity and the results you get—beliefs.

Every person is the creation of himself,
the image of his own thinking and believing.
As individuals think and believe, so they are.
—Claude M. Bristol

Chapter Two

Belief—
Well, if You Say So

Your belief that you can do the thing
gives your thought forces their power.
—Robert Collier

Belief creates the actual fact.
—William James

T hink of identity as a building. Beliefs are the bricks that it is built with. We all know we have beliefs, but beyond that we don't really think much about them. Nonetheless, beliefs are incredibly important when it comes to shaping our lives in both the short-term and the long-term, whether these beliefs are positive or negative.

We Act on Our Beliefs About Reality, Not on Reality Itself
As much as we hear these days of the importance of "keeping it real," when it comes to getting results, reality has a lot less to do with it than you might realize. This is because people don't perform based on their abilities nearly so much as they perform based on what they *believe* their abilities to be. If this sounds strange, it will make a lot more sense by the end of this chapter.

A belief is a sense of certainty, a sense of "this is the way it is." Beliefs act as filters on our experience. Like tinted glasses, our beliefs color our perception of everything coming in from the outside world. Our minds act on our interpretation of something, not the actual thing or experience itself. (Like the idea of seeing results in advance, this is a major point and is going to keep coming up, so let it settle in.) As an example, let's say you are walking down a path in the woods and out of the corner of your eye you see a piece of rope that you believe is a snake. What do you think you are going to react to, the reality that it is a piece of rope or the belief that it is a snake? You are going to react as if it is a snake and you will jump back before you have a chance to see that it is only rope. We do not react to what is going on. We react to what we *believe* is going on. Always.

In the province of the mind,
what one believes to be true either is true or becomes true.
—John Lilly

Maybe you've heard of Harry Houdini, the legendary magician and escape artist. In promoting his act, Houdini would arrive in the town where he was to perform, insisting that there was no cell that could hold him, no lock he could not conquer within an hour. As the story goes, there was a little town in England that took up the challenge and invited him to stake his claim by testing their "escape-proof" cell.

So, he arrives at the jail and into the cell he goes. As soon as the door is shut behind him, he goes to work on breaking out. As time passes and his usual tricks aren't getting the job done, he is starting to sweat. After the hour is up, the jailer returns to find Houdini sitting silently in defeat. To Houdini's amazement and shame, the jailer simply opened the door and let him out. It had never been locked in the first place.

How is it that the world's greatest magician and escape artist could not escape from an unlocked cell? To make sense of this, you need to realize that it isn't the events, situations, or conditions that mold our lives, but how we interpret them that is the key. In other words, the things that happen to us aren't nearly as important as the meaning we attach to them. And it is our beliefs that determine what meaning we give things.

Experience is not what happens to a man.
It is what a man does with what happens to him.
—Aldous Huxley

Your Beliefs Direct Your Behavior
As an example, let me tell you about a student I once had. Matt was off the wall during the first semester of his freshman year. He was friendly, he was enthusiastic, and he was failing. He just couldn't get his priorities straight. As he started to take a nose-dive, he saw everything coming through his belief-tinted window as just one more reason why he would not be able to make the grade. He saw a few F's and began to see things in that light. After this, when he received an assignment, he expected to fail, or at least do a rotten job on it. And of course he was right, because our beliefs determine the direction in which our behavior will go. So he failed, and so would you if you believed the way he did.

The interesting thing about Matt, though, was that he got another idea at the beginning of the second semester. After a few heart to heart talks, I got the idea through to him that he could not only pass, but that he could get an A. He didn't believe it at first, but with enough good-natured badgering from me, he began to believe, and he began to get psyched.

Matt got the idea that he wanted an A for the second semester. Not what he should do, not what he was expected to do, but what he wanted to do. It wasn't someone on the outside pushing him to do it. It was all him. You can imagine how that changed things. Now, when he received an assignment, getting an A on it was of the utmost importance. He had a goal and he was committed to achieving it. Instead of expecting to fail and doing all of the things that would insure failure, such as procrastinating or not bothering to do the assignment at all, he was determined to do it right, and right away. Also, he would ask for help whenever he didn't understand something. With getting an A being so important to him, his whole outlook changed. He was excited about school, and he would ask about his grade constantly, making sure that he was maintaining it. Since he was an athlete, he turned schoolwork into a competition and translated his athletic success into academic success.

With such attention and determination to meet his goal, he did wind up getting an A, which made him feel great. But the lasting benefit beyond his immediate grade was his confidence in his ability. When it came time to register for his classes the following year, instead of taking the easier English class (which had been his plan), he decided to build upon his success and take the more challenging class.

What happened here? Matt didn't get any smarter between semesters, and I was grading him the same way I had been previously. He was in the same class, with the same teacher giving the same kind of assignments. How did he go from failing to getting an A? The only difference was the attitude that Matt brought with him to class. His beliefs changed, and then his performance followed his beliefs. Remember, the beliefs you have will direct the results you consistently get. It's law of human behavior.

> *Man is not the creature of circumstances.*
> *Circumstances are the creatures of men.*
> —*Benjamin Disraeli*

A Little Belief is Stronger than an Elephant

But you know what? It's not only humans. To see just how controlling beliefs can be, consider elephants. You know elephants, the smartest animal in the jungle and all that. Here's how they're trained in India. When an elephant is just a baby, its owner secures one of its ankles with a heavy chain fastened to a large stake in the ground because left unrestrained, a baby elephant is going to go everywhere and get into everything. (Think of it as a kitten on steroids.) The elephant tries to go beyond the area allowed by the chain, but can't. So it tugs and tugs and tugs. After repeated attempts that go nowhere, it becomes discouraged and quits.

But here's the weird part. As the elephant grows and gets stronger and stronger, instead of using heavier chains, which would seem to make sense, its owner switches from chains to heavy rope, and then gradually to lighter and lighter rope. By the time the elephant is fully grown and is strong enough to knock over a house, a thin rope tied to a broom handle stuck in the ground is all that is needed to keep it restrained. Why? Because its belief (through past experience) that it cannot free itself constricts its true potential and determines the results that it will get. Because of past difficulties, a grown elephant allows itself be restrained without making any effort at all. It just gives up.

Can you see now why it doesn't matter whether or not a belief is based in reality? If a mighty elephant believes it cannot break a rope that in reality it could snap in a second, it's absolutely right—it can't! The problem is that many of us are just like elephants. We are operating under beliefs formed long ago, beliefs that we have allowed to shape our lives in limiting ways. Your beliefs control how much of your resources you will use in any given situation. Your mind will direct your behavior in the direction of your belief.

What Kind of Programs are You Running in Your Computer?

Let's go back to our earlier analogy of the mind being like a computer. Beliefs are like software. If you work with a computer, you know that it is the program that determines what the computer does. Your mind is the same way—whatever program (belief) you run will go a long way in determining what you get out of it.

If you are not succeeding at the moment, it is quite possible that you are running disempowering or limiting programs in your computer. The constant "I can't do it," "I'm not smart enough," "I'm too lazy," "I'm just not like that," "I don't have the time"—if this kind of stuff gets programmed in, you are generally going to get results that are in line with these beliefs. Your mind is extremely efficient; it gives you exactly what you put into it on a consistent basis. If you want to get new results consistently, you have to program in new beliefs. The good news is that this is not that difficult to do, once you know how.

But what if you don't believe it? Look, I don't want to be mean, but if you don't believe that it is possible to make any of the necessary changes, you *won't* make them—just like the elephant we talked about. But doesn't this just show how strong belief can be? So give yourself a chance to use the very power you are using right now to disbelieve you can do something and turn it around. This is called the willing suspension of disbelief. You just put your disbelief on hold long enough to have an open mind and check out the possibilities. If it does turn out that you were correct the whole time and everything I am saying here is garbage, you can always go back to where you were when you started, right?

In the meantime, if you don't believe that you can get A's or better grades in general, if you're saying to yourself that this sounds good for somebody else, but you have been getting F's or C's or whatever, and you're just not good enough or smart enough, you must remember that getting the grades isn't anywhere near as much a matter of being smart enough than it is of getting rid of the baggage that has been programmed into your mind. Get rid of that negative baggage and replace it with the belief that you *can* do it, and you will be on your way to accomplishing your goal.

But please realize that this isn't because belief is some kind of hocus-pocus magic wand that you can wave and that is that. You will be on your way to accomplishing your goal because once you shift the beliefs that are holding you back, you allow yourself the opportunity to use the power and resources *you already have.* Not using something is a lot different than not having something, isn't it? Yet far too often, people believe they don't possess a trait or skill they actually do possess, but just aren't using. However, if it turns out that you are lacking in necessary skills or resources, the shifting of the limiting belief will help you in your ability to acquire what you need.

The results you get fall in line with the programs you are running and you *can* change them. This what Matt did, and it's what you can do as well. Also, like Matt, you've got to realize that you don't necessarily have to settle for progress in small steps. It would have been easy for Matt to work toward getting a D, since that would seem like the logical place to begin if he was failing. But it doesn't have to work that way. Matt didn't go for a D. He jumped from an F to an A in one step. You can make large leaps in progress as well, skipping over the "logical" steps in between, *if* you adjust your beliefs and identity to the new level you wish to operate on. It can happen, and it does happen for people who are willing to put these techniques to work.

Man is made or unmade by himself. In the armory of thought
he forges the weapons by which he destroys himself.
He also fashions the tools with which he builds for himself
heavenly mansions of joy and strength and peace.
—James Allen

Beliefs are Established by Conditioning

Now that you have some understanding of how beliefs guide you and the value of running positive programs to get positive results, what do you do if you have some rotten beliefs already programmed in? Just saying, "I don't believe that stuff anymore" and leaving it at that isn't going to be enough, because once your beliefs are programmed in, they become unconscious.

Beliefs are just like anything else—they are reinforced through conditioning, or practice. How do you learn how to do anything? Through repetition, right? Do something over and over and it becomes second nature. This is because the repetition of an action establishes pathways in your nervous system that are called neural pathways. The more established these pathways become, the more "automatic" an action or behavior becomes. This is how both good and bad habits are developed, and anything you now do without thinking about it has come about in this way. Developing a belief is similar to developing a habit.

If you want a perfect example of how this process works, think of tying your shoe. How long does it take? Probably three or four seconds, right? Also, you don't have to pay close attention to what you are doing because it's something you do every day without even thinking about it. Your "shoe-tying" pathway is deeply established in your nervous system.

But try something different. Instead of doing it the normal way, do everything the opposite way. In other words, if you normally start by wrapping the left-hand lace over the right-hand lace, do it the other way around. If you make the loop with your right hand and wrap the left-hand lace around it before pulling it through, reverse the process by making the loop with the left hand, etc. The first thing you will notice is that this easy, everyday routine just became something you really have to concentrate on—if you can do it at all. The reason for this is simple. Even though you are doing something that is similar to the way you normally do it, the neural pathway for this new variation has not been established, so you have to pay close attention to every step of the process.

What do you think would happen if you started tying your shoes like this every day? At first, it would be clumsy and you would have to pay a lot of attention to what you were doing. But after awhile, it would begin to feel natural. You wouldn't be thinking about it at all—it would just be the way you tied your shoes. But you know what? The old way, the way that you had been tying your shoes all these years, would feel strange and you would have to concentrate in order to do it. Your old "shoe-tying" neural pathway would become weakened through neglect and a new one would be established in its place.

As you may have guessed, this principle works with beliefs, too. Ultimately, if you practice, it's as simple as tying your shoes.

How to Change a Belief

So how do you change a disempowering belief into one that will enable you to get the kind of results you are after?

One: Decide you must change this belief

This is important because if you don't feel that you *must* change this belief, you won't be motivated to actually work on changing, and you will fall back into your old patterns when the novelty of the new idea wears off. (And it always does.) Remember, just as your habits are programmed into your nervous system like software, your beliefs are programmed into your mind. If you don't change the program, the old one will keep running. (This is what is happening when you try to change, but just can't seem to stop yourself from continuing to do the exact thing you set out to change.)

When you decide that you are going to change, you set yourself on a new path. With determination, you can keep moving in the right direction until you have established your new belief to the point where you don't even have to think about it anymore—it's the way you are. (Beliefs are the bricks you use to build your identity.)

Two: Attach great pain to the old belief

You want to understand (and *feel*) specifically and in detail, exactly what your old belief will cost you now and in the future if you don't change it. For example, what is the price of living beneath the weight of a belief that you are lazy? Or the belief that you can never do well on tests? Or the belief that you always procrastinate? Or the belief that absolutely everything about school is boring? Or any negative belief that you can isolate?

It's easy to just say, "that sucks!" And you're right—it does suck. But so what? The point is to get yourself to feel like you really need to change this belief, to get it out of your way so that you can achieve greater things than you are right now. Just saying "that sucks!" isn't good enough to get the job done. But if you want to get some motivation to move yourself in a different direction, here's something that can help you do so.

If you find yourself wanting to skip this part, that is understandable. Admittedly, it isn't a lot of fun. But that's the point—it shows you upfront the effect that the negative belief can have on your ability to accomplish what you want to accomplish. So if you want to see this up close and personal, take the necessary time and write out *in detail* what this belief (or beliefs) is doing to your life. What results are you going to miss out on if you keep this belief? What opportunities are you going to pass up? (We're not just talking about school here; we're talking about your life as a whole.) Feel what it is like to live in such a limiting way. Do you like it? What do you think you will be like in five years if you are still living with this belief? In ten years?

Again, write it out in detail so you can see the results that living under the weight of this limiting belief will bring you. You might want to rely on your memory to do this, but it's not as effective because it will fade. It's a lot better to get hard evidence in writing. It may not be fun to do, but it *will* show you the price you are paying by letting this belief control your life. And how much fun is that?

Of course, you might be wondering why I am asking you to make yourself feel bad on purpose, but it *is* beneficial to attach a lot of pain to your old belief. This sounds crazy at first, but it makes sense if you think about it. Look at it like a toothache. When you have one, it causes you a lot of suffering because it hurts all the time. When you go to the dentist and he pulls it out, that hurts, too. But when he's done, you don't have that rotten tooth causing all of that pain in your head. The short-term pain is worthwhile because it gets rid of the long-term pain. It's the same with your limiting belief. Confronting where it is actually leading you is painful, but doing so helps you pull that rotten belief out of your head. It takes away the long-term suffering you would have had to put up with if you had just left that rotten belief festering there without taking any action.

None of us likes to do things that are painful, do we? Even when we are doing things that others think are painful, we are getting some form of pleasure out of them, right? Virtually all of our actions can be boiled down to this simple formula: we move away from pain and move toward pleasure. It's human nature, and it's how our minds work. So if we attach a lot of pain to our old belief, we will naturally want to move away from it.

Three: Attach great pleasure to the new belief

If you are going to move away from your old, limiting, painful belief, you need something to move toward. Figure out what the opposite of your old belief is. If, for example, you are being limited by a belief that you are lazy, you might want to work with the new belief that you are a hard worker. Or, if you are constantly telling yourself that you procrastinate, work with the new belief that you do what needs to be done as soon as it needs to be done.

Once you have your new belief, take the time and write out *in detail* all of the benefits that you will gain by adopting this new belief and making it a part of you. What results are you going to obtain if you install this belief? What opportunities are you going to go for? *Feel* what it is like to live in such an empowering way. Do you like it? Do you think you will like what five or ten years of living with this belief will bring you? Make these feelings of accomplishment as attractive as possible. Give yourself compelling reasons to move in this new and powerful direction. Don't just haphazardly think about it or write a sentence or two. This shouldn't be an assignment you resist doing because, unlike the last part, this one isn't painful. Do whatever you can to make it pleasurable because you are going a long way toward creating your success, right here, right now. I know it looks like just a couple of lists, but there's a lot more to it, *if* you follow through.

Look at what you have written about your disempowering belief side by side with what you wrote about your empowering belief. Which path is more attractive? Which one do you want to head down? The choice really is yours.

Four: Install the new belief into your mind's computer
This step has to do with the concept of visualizing, or seeing your desired results in advance, and it is the subject of our next chapter.

Beliefs Filter Out Contrary Evidence
Before closing this chapter, however, I want to touch on an objection that you might have with this whole procedure. Look, it's easy to say that you are lying to yourself if you pretend to believe something about yourself before you have any evidence to back it up. But you shouldn't worry about this; I am not asking you to lie to yourself or about yourself. I am asking you to take a closer look at your situation. You see, beliefs filter out everything that doesn't fit within their borders. What happens frequently is that a person laboring under a particular belief will ignore, or fail to notice, any evidence to the contrary.

For example, I had a student who had difficulty getting her schoolwork done most of the time. When asked why, she would smile and say, "oh, I'm just lazy." This same student happened to be a star swimmer, and she could be found working on her swimming for hours each day. But because this obvious evidence of hard work did not fit into her belief that she was lazy, she ignored it as if it didn't apply. If she were to change her "I'm lazy" belief into "I'm a hard worker," she could then access all of this evidence and use it for her studies or whatever else she was interested in besides swimming.

Regardless of your belief, you probably have evidence from your life that contradicts the limitations you are placing on yourself. Face it, there are plenty of times when you don't procrastinate, times when you feel great, enjoy being at school, enjoy reading, or whatever. In all but the most extreme cases, these times *are* there. You've got to focus on them. Yet, far too often, we just won't do it, convinced we know what's what.

I remember a summer school student who was a perfect example of someone who wasn't seeing the possibilities of what she could do. On the first day of class, I used to give out a questionnaire to help me get to know my students a little bit. One of the first questions was, "What do you hate about English class?" Well, this student said that she hated everything about English class, *especially* writing. So what did she do during every free moment in class? You might think that she talked to her classmates, but that wasn't it. She spent her whole time writing page after page of letters to her friends. Since I hadn't assigned it, she didn't consider it "writing" because she liked doing it and could write whatever she wanted.

The point is that you almost always have evidence or experience to support your new belief. It's just that you've been too busy focusing on the support for your old belief to notice.

Create Evidence for Your New Belief

But let's say you've searched high and low and you just don't have any support for your new belief. Does this mean you cannot develop it and are only lying to yourself? No. Certainly, you can develop your new belief. All you have to do is go out and get some evidence right now. For example, if you have a new belief that you are a hard worker, go do some work and do it well. When you finish, you can say to yourself, "see, I *am* a hard worker." It sounds like I am joking, but I'm not. If you have evidence that you can work hard and are willing to work at conditioning your new belief, you will be on your way to establishing a new belief and getting the kind of results that go along with it. Just like that.

The important thing to realize is that yesterday doesn't make any difference—*if* you are getting results today. Usually, however, we aren't willing to give ourselves a chance because we get stuck in dwelling on what we have been doing or not doing in the past, and this isn't right.

Tomorrow is Not Chained to Yesterday

As an example, say I've been smoking cigarettes and decide to quit. No matter how long I've been smoking, the day I quit, I am no longer a smoker, even if I've been smoking for twenty years before that. If I were to tell someone that I'd quit and they said, "no you haven't, you've been smoking for twenty years," it would be pretty stupid for me to say, "I guess you're right, I'm just lying to myself. I guess I'll always be a smoker." But that's what we do to ourselves if we say we can't be hard workers, or get our work done on time, or do well on tests, or whatever, if we haven't been doing so up to this point. If you truly decide to change and work to program in your new belief, yesterday is beside the point. Unless you want to be like the elephant.

What can or cannot be done is determined largely by our beliefs. Of course, it cuts both ways. When you think something cannot be done, you're right—it cannot. Here is an excellent example from a player in the National Football League who was asked what was wrong with his team's offense, one that had been quite good the year before but had fallen on hard times in the new season: "This is the same offense that last year set a franchise record for points. Nobody is missing. Right now, as far as an offensive unit, we've got to believe. I think that's what is missing. We don't believe in each other. We don't believe that person can make a play anymore. I think in the past we used to go out on the field thinking that at any given time, somebody was going to make a play. . . . I just think now we don't believe."

Think you can or think you can't.
Either way you are right.
—*Henry Ford*

To Dream the Impossible Dream

When you think something *can* be done, your belief drives you to use your resources to a far greater extent, and things that may have appeared impossible become possible indeed. An excellent example of the impossible becoming possible through belief is the story of Roger Bannister. It was 1954, and for all of the years that people had been timing runners, it was believed that no one would ever be able to run the mile in under four minutes. In fact, the standard medical opinion was that it was physically impossible; the human body just couldn't handle the strain. But Roger Bannister wanted to do it anyway. So he trained intensely, believing all the while that it *could* be done.

Of course, he did go on to become the first person to do it. Such is the power of belief. But an even more impressive testimony to the power of belief soon followed. This barrier of the four-minute mile, a barrier that had stood for so long and was seen as an impossibility, was broken again by a different runner just forty-six days later, and by *thirty-seven* runners in the following year. All because one determined runner believed that it wasn't impossible after all. Other runners saw a man achieve the "impossible," so they installed the new belief that they could do it as well. And they were right.

While they were saying among themselves it cannot be done,
it was done.
—*Helen Keller*

Believe it can be done. When you believe something can be done,
really believe, your mind will find the ways to do it.
—*David J. Schwartz*

Chapter Three

Visualization—
As If

*If one advances confidently in the direction of his dreams,
and endeavors to live the life that he has imagined,
he will meet with a success unexpected in common hours.*
—Henry David Thoreau

In the last chapter, I said that step four of our formula for changing beliefs was to install your new belief by working to see the results of your new belief in advance. If you will remember, this concept was mentioned briefly in our discussion about identity. Since beliefs are the bricks identity is made of, what works for identity will also work for beliefs.

Visualizing is a Mark of Successful People in All Fields
Success isn't an accident or luck, regardless of what some folks think. There are definite qualities that foster it, and one trait that successful people in all fields share is the ability to *see* themselves achieving their goals *before* they set out achieve them, of seeing results in advance. This concept has different names: imaging, mental scripting, mental rehearsal, mental mapping, visualization, etc. Whatever the name, it's the same principle. If you want

to be more successful as a student or in anything else, you will be doing yourself a tremendous favor if you develop the habit of visualizing in advance the results you want to achieve. In short, *begin with the end in mind.* Literally.

When a thought is made dynamic by will force,
it can manifest according to the mental blueprint you have created.
—*Paramahansa Yogananda*

Your Mind Responds to a Strongly Imagined Idea as if It Were Real

Think of when you are falling asleep at night and you start to dream just as you begin drifting off. What happens when you dream of, say, somebody throwing something at you? Your arm flinches or your head jerks while you are lying there and you wake up. This happens because, when it comes to reacting to something, your mind *can't tell the difference* between reality and imagination—*if* the imagination is strong enough. It really can't. Like I said in the last chapter, we don't react to what is going on, but to what we believe is going on. Always.

We just mentioned Roger Bannister's achievement and its effect on other runners, which is a testimony to the power of belief. But, as usual, there's more to the story. Bannister knew that in order to attain his goal, he would have to train as hard mentally as he did physically. One of the things he did was run the race in his mind, step by step, lap by lap, seeing himself finishing the race in less than four minutes. He did this constantly, even though he was still unable to actually do so on the track, and it prepared his mind to accept the possibility of actually doing it during a real race. When you strongly imagine something, your mind takes this as an indication of the direction you want to move in, and it begins moving you in that direction because, as I said, it can't tell the difference between a strongly imagined idea and reality.

Picture yourself vividly as winning
and that alone will contribute immeasurably to your success.
Great living starts with a picture held in your imagination
of what you would like to do or be.
—*Harry Emerson Fosdick*

Of course, Bannister isn't the only athlete to have worked on visualizing results. Many athletes from all sports routinely go through this process. It is an important part of their training. Barry Bonds, of the San Francisco Giants, has said that in order to prepare himself for the next game, he visualizes the opposing pitcher's delivery and the spin of the ball, as well as how he will need to react in order to have a successful at bat against that pitcher. As most baseball fans know, Barry Bonds is considered by many to be the best hitter of his generation, if not the greatest of all-time.

We All Visualize, But Too Often for Negative Results

Of course, if this stuff just worked for athletes, there wouldn't be much point in bringing it up here, would there? But remember, a key trait of successful people in all fields is their ability to see the results they want in advance. By conditioning their mind in this way, they reach the point where they *expect* to succeed.

This expectation, as we said in the chapter on identity, makes all of the difference. Sadly, however, many people expect to fail in most situations and spend the majority of their mental energy going over and over their fears and expectations of this failure. When they eventually do fail, their response is along the lines of, "see, I *knew* it!" I've seen this happen with students again and again. Before a test, they quietly whip themselves into a state of mind that allows them little chance of success because it is thoroughly focused on failure, and most of the time, they do fail.

Well, of course they do—look at what's going on here. They've become experts at exactly what I'm talking about. They are seeing results in advance, but they're seeing rotten results.

> *See the things you want as already yours.*
> *Think of them as yours, as belonging to you,*
> *as already in your possession.*
> —*Robert Collier*

Say you are one of these students who habitually expects to do poorly. What if you were to use the same habit that you already have, but instead of using it to get negative results, you used it to produce positive results? You *can* do this. There's no rule that says you have to always expect to do poorly, even if you have done so up to this point. Think of it this way: Past failures are like mud you've walked through, and the present is like a brand new carpet. Guess what? Nobody wants you tromping your muddy boots all across this beautiful carpet. So how about taking them off?

Stop Being so "Realistic"

But if you are one of those folks who will insist that you are "just being realistic," I've got a few questions. Why is it that, with few exceptions, whenever someone is "just being realistic," they are being negative or trying to excuse why something cannot be done? Why is it that "being realistic" is never positive? Why is it that "being realistic" is invariably an effort to put the brakes on some kind of progress, dream, or goal?

It is difficult to say what is impossible,
for the dream of yesterday is the hope of today
and the reality of tomorrow.
—Robert H. Goddard

Take a look around at all of the everyday things that we take for granted—the cars, the planes, the televisions, the telephones, the computers and so on. Not a single one of these inventions, along with countless others, was "realistic" at the time they were being worked on. And you can be sure that every step of the way there was someone whispering in the ear of the inventor or creator, trying to talk them out of whatever they were doing, all the time insisting they were "just being realistic."

As an example of how limiting this "realistic" talk can be, think of a toilet. Can you believe that when it was first being introduced there were some people who were "just being realistic" when they pointed out that it would be insane idea to believe that people would actually want something like a toilet in their house? After all, that was something you took care of outside, away from where you lived.

Another thing about these inventions and everything else that you see out there in the "real" world is that there isn't anything that's been built, invented, or created that hasn't first been imagined in the mind. Everything comes from the mind, which is why you shouldn't worry so much about the "real" world in this regard. After all, the majority of your life doesn't take place there, anyway. It takes place between your ears, and what you are consistently doing *in there* largely determines what will happen on the outside, because your beliefs filter your experience of what's "real." So forget about being "realistic." When it's used in this way, it's just a code word for lowering your expectations and settling for less.

The world is moving so fast nowadays
that the man who says it can't be done
is generally interrupted by someone doing it.
—*Elbert Hubbard*

In Which Direction are You Going?

Whether we succeed or whether we fail is largely determined by how we spend our mental time. We are always thinking about something or other, and our thoughts generally fall into habitual patterns. As I said, successful people expect successful results, and spend much of their mental effort visualizing these successful results in advance. They're using the same technique that unsuccessful people are using, but they're pointing it in a positive direction instead of a negative direction. That's why positive visualization is such an excellent practice. When you do it consistently, with concentration and deep feeling, the message that is sent to your mind is, "I'm doing it now, so I will be able to do it later as well." Since you are going to be visualizing anyway, in which direction do you want your mental effort to point?

This is the role visualization plays in the achievement process: Know exactly what you are going for, **consistently see yourself as having already accomplished it**, fully expect that you will do so, and feel that way.

Losers visualize the penalties of failure.
Winners visualize the rewards of success.
—*Robert Gilbert*

The Steps for Changing a Belief in Review

So how do you practice visualizing when it comes to your new belief? Let's quickly review the first three steps of changing your disempowering belief.

The first step was to determine what belief you wanted to get rid of and decide, once and for all, that you weren't going to be ruled by this belief anymore. Remember, without this determination, you risk falling back into the old belief due to the fact that it is already programmed into your mind.

The second step was to attach lots of pain to your old belief. This is necessary because we move away from pain and toward pleasure. If you can really *feel* that your old belief and the results it brings you are painful, then you will naturally want to move away from it.

The third step was to determine your new, empowering belief and attach a lot of pleasure to it. This is necessary because you need something to move toward while you are moving away from your old belief. By attaching a lot of pleasure to the new belief and the results it will bring, you give your mind a reason to move in that direction.

The fourth step is to begin programming your new belief into your mind. I said that it was important to find some evidence from past experience to back up your new belief, and that if that wasn't possible, to go and get some evidence in the present. Of course, you will also want practice visualizing, or seeing results in advance.

Preliminary Visualization Points

Here are some points that will help you get the most out of your visualization practice. First, if it seems kind of funny in the beginning, don't worry. The more you do it the better you get at it, and the better you get, the better your results and the more you will be willing to do it.

It would be good if you could be in a quiet place where you can work without being bothered for least five or ten minutes so you can concentrate on what you are doing without being interrupted. Before you go to bed or when you get up are both excellent times, but you can do it anytime you have a few minutes to spare.

You'll want to be comfortable and in a position where you can relax. Lying down is ok, but many people find it too easy to drift off to sleep. If this presents a problem for you, try sitting in a comfortable chair. Close your eyes and take a few slow, deep breaths until you are feeling calm. The greater the state of relaxation you can get into, the better your results will be because the deeper you will go into your subconscious.

When you do your visualization, work to make it as complete as possible, filling in as many details as you can from the surroundings you are placing yourself in. For example, if you are working on a situation for a certain class, see yourself in that classroom as best as you can. If it is something connected with a sport, put yourself on the court or field, etc. This may seem difficult at first, but as you practice, you will get better. The more "real" you can make your visualization, the more your mind will be compelled to move you in that direction because, as far as it is concerned, you *are* moving in that direction.

Think What You Will, But to Feel is for Real

But what if you are one of those people who just can't visualize very well? Let's face it, some folks can make pictures in their heads really well, others cannot. If, like me, you are one of the ones who can't, don't worry. For all of the talk of "visualizing," "imaging," or "seeing" results in advance, the pictures by themselves are not the most important part of the process. Certainly they are beneficial, but the most critical element by far, is the feeling that you generate *while* you are visualizing. The images you create set the scene, but the feelings you feel while you are doing so drive it all home. So if you can't make great pictures, just do the best that you can and concentrate on the feelings that would be present in such a situation. Even if you are quite good at making pictures, you *still* want to focus on the feelings that go along with the pictures you are creating.

I've run into quite a few people who have sought to dismiss visualization or any kind mental training by saying something along the lines of, "oh, that's just that positive thinking stuff. I tried it and it didn't work." And maybe it didn't work, but there's a good reason why it didn't. You can do all the positive thinking, all the affirmations, and all the visualizations you want and still not get the results you are after. This is not because it doesn't work, but because it doesn't work *alone.*

In a nutshell, feeling has more influence than thinking. If you are thinking one thing and feeling the opposite, the feeling has a much greater chance of carrying the day. In other words, if your thoughts are saying, "I can, I can, I can," and your feelings are going, "not really, not really, not really," guess what? Feeling trumps thought. This is why fear is such a killer, and why it is so important to focus on how you would feel if you were to achieve the results you are visualizing. Yes, make the pictures as big and bright as you can, but don't forget to feel how you would feel if you were experiencing the scene you are visualizing.

This is the role feeling plays in the achievement process: Know exactly what you are going for, consistently see yourself as having already accomplished it, fully expect that you will do so, **and feel that way.**

Think and feel yourself there!
To achieve any aim in life, you need to project the end-result.
Think of the elation, the satisfaction, the joy!
Carrying the ecstatic feeling will bring the desired goal into view.
—*Grace Speare*

A Hard-Working Example

Ok, let's run through an example and see how this works. Say you've been having trouble getting your work done, or you do it, but you don't put much effort into it. If this is a normal situation for you, you are probably running some version of the program, "I'm not a good worker because I'm lazy." This belief gets you the kind of results that you'd rather not brag about. A good belief to use instead of this disempowering one is, "I am a hard worker, and I get the job done." I definitely needed to program this one for myself in order to get over a dominant belief of being lazy, a belief that was routinely holding me back from getting any real work done and had hurt me for years. If you want physical proof that the elements of achievement really do work, look no further than this book you are holding in your hands. I could never have seen this project through if it weren't for the concepts and practices that I am teaching you right here.

Take your new belief and think of a situation where it would apply. For example, imagine a type of assignment that you are likely to receive, one that has caused you difficulty in the past. Visualize yourself getting that assignment. Are you going to be like most students? Are you going to approach it with resistance and the expectation of struggling through it, miserable and whining about how mean the teacher is for giving it? *No.* You are a hard worker, and hard workers attack their assignments with enthusiasm; they don't waste their time trying to get out of doing it and they don't waste their energy on whether or not they like the assignment, the subject, or the teacher. (This is why they always seem to be half finished when the others are just getting started.)

See yourself in your imagination starting your assignment immediately after receiving it. No resisting, no complaining, you pull a Nike and *just do it.* Feel the good feeling that comes from knowing that you are again about to successfully accomplish something. See yourself working hard to finish your task. See yourself working steadily; you're not rushing just to get it done. Feel how good it feels knowing that you attacked it with gusto and put in the necessary effort to do a good job. Feel the confidence that comes from such an effort, confidence that you can apply to any area you choose because hard work in one area translates to hard work in other areas as well. After all, you *are* a hard worker; it's just the way you are.

See yourself getting an A on the assignment. Feel how good it is to be getting A's consistently. See yourself bringing home a report card with straight A's. How does it feel to hand a report card like this to your folks? How does it feel to have them be so proud of you? How does it feel to know that your hard work has brought you yet another success? How does it feel for *you* to be proud of yourself? (Believe it or not, it can take some getting used to.) Feel these positive feelings deeply because these feelings of success and pride are the result of the fact that *you* are a hard worker who gets the job done.

Repeat this process daily for a couple of minutes, using different situations and emphasizing the fact that you are a hard worker who gets the job done (or whatever belief you are working with) and feeling how good it feels to be accomplishing so much more than you were before. The more intensely you can feel the results, the more you can tie them to positive emotions, the deeper they will go into your mind. Since it's *your* imagination, you can do anything you want in there, be anyone you want to be, right? The more intense you make it in there, the more you move in that direction out here.

Dreams have as much influence as actions.
—Stephane Mallarme

Visualization Plants Seeds of Success

Remember, when it comes to reacting, your mind doesn't know the difference between doing something for real and your vividly imagining yourself doing something. So if you work with concentration and feeling (just like so many great athletes and other professionals do), you are taking advantage of this fact, and you are mentally training. This repetition on the mental level will greatly assist you in your actual acquisition of the skills or beliefs that you want to acquire.

Visualization is like planting seeds—you are going to harvest what you plant. By planting positive, deliberate images of success in your mind, you are preparing yourself for a successful harvest. Of course, this isn't hocus-pocus; it isn't magic. You still have to do the work along the way, just as you do when you plant a garden. But if you are consistently working on your visualization in line with your new belief, you will see that you begin to get similar results in real life, and you will start thinking of yourself in terms of your new belief, which is how visualization connects with identity.

This identification with your new belief will lead you to get better at your visualization, and that in turn will make you want to work toward achieving the same results for real because you will know how good it feels to be successful and in control of the direction in which your life is going. Getting results is a lot more fun than sitting around complaining about how you're bored, or how much school sucks. As you build up momentum, you will get more and more evidence for your new belief. Soon, you won't have to consciously work on it because it will be a stable part of who you are. Imagine how good *that* feels!

Envisioning the end is enough to put the means in motion.
—*Dorothea Brande*

What is now proved was once only imagined.
—*William Blake*

One's life is dyed in the color of his imagination.
—*Marcus Aurelius*

Chapter Four

Goals—
If You Don't Know Where You Are Going,
How Will You Know When You Get There?

There is no achievement without goals.
—Robert J. McKain

Man is a goal-seeking animal.
His life only has meaning
if he is reaching out and striving for his goals.
—Aristotle

Visualization is a wonderful technique for helping you to condition your new beliefs. It is also a great way to help you condition your identity to fall in line with the kinds of results you want to achieve. But what results do you want to achieve? What are you going for? "Well, that's easy. I want to get better grades, and I want to be a better student." These are good things to want, but they're a little vague, aren't they? In order to help you get better results faster, we need to spend some time with another trait that successful people of all stripes share: the ability to set specific goals. As I said in the last chapter, anything that has been created by anyone—any invention, building, game, work of art, software program, organization, or whatever, has started out in the imagination as a dream and, therefore, had to be a goal before it came into physical being as a successful achievement. If you really are serious about being successful in your schoolwork or any other pursuit you are interested in, you will surely want to understand the power of goal setting.

However necessary goals are to success, they do seem to frighten a lot of folks, and many people keep their dreams vague on purpose. It's as if they think they might get lucky and sneak up on these dreams, or that they can sneak away quietly without any commitment if things don't work out. But this haphazard approach is not the approach that you want to take. Successful is not an accident, and it isn't luck. If you want to succeed, you need to plan for it because if you don't, you are planning for something else.

Failing to plan is planning to fail.
—Anonymous

Goals Carry You Through Failures and Keep You on Track
One of the most common objections to setting specific goals is, "what if I set a goal and then fail to achieve it? Aren't I just setting myself up to be disappointed?" True, there is risk involved, but there's always some risk involved in any achievement, isn't there?

One doesn't discover new lands
without consenting to lose sight of the shore for a very long time.
—Andre Gide

We all like security. But in order to reach new heights, we've got to take some risks. It's just like in baseball: You can't steal second with one foot on first, can you? Unless you're willing to never go for anything at all for the rest of your life, you are going to have to take some chances, right? And some of these chances are not going to work out. Well, so what? Nobody succeeds without failing a lot along the way. The difference between the winner and the loser is that the winner gets up and keeps on going, while the loser stays down and quits. It's not falling down you want to worry about, but whether or not you get back up. Goals give you a reason to get up again. You fall down, you get up. No big deal.

Failure is only the opportunity to begin again more intelligently.
—Henry Ford

We All Have Goals, But Where are They Leading Us?

A great thing about goals is their ability to keep you on track. Without specific, consciously chosen goals you can wander aimlessly for years, never knowing where you are going, or what's around the next corner. As bad as that sounds, it's normal. Wandering around is the way a lot of people spend their lives. If you look around, you can see that most people are not satisfied with the quality of the life they're living. Are you?

Although I'm putting special emphasis on goals at this point, I'm not implying that they are something brand new for you; they are already a regular part of everyone's life. After all, we're all chasing something, aren't we? No matter what we are doing, we are trying to achieve something. Even the student who just sits there every day staring into space or sleeping is pursuing something, even if it's just getting through the day without having to do anything or be bothered by anyone. But these short-term goals are not the same as the specific, long-range goals you want to learn to develop. Like everything else in this book, it's a matter of learning to use the skills you already have in a more positively focused way. It's about taking conscious control of the skills you've been using unconsciously all along.

Goals Let You See Past Distractions and Obstacles

One big difference between someone who chronically fails and someone who is successful is that the person who is failing generally has only short-range goals that are easily set aside whenever any old whim comes along. The successful person generally has long-range, specific goals that carry him or her through distractions and problems.

Goals drive your actions. When you have a definite, specific direction in which you are moving, you are able to see beyond temporary obstacles by keeping your eyes on your goal. Without goals, every little problem that comes up can affect you greatly because without the long-range vision that goals provide, the problem is all that you can see.

For example, as a student, there are going to be times when you will not like the subject, the class, or the teacher. This is just the way it goes. But what happens to most students in this situation is that they get sidetracked by this dislike and do poorly in the class. If you ask them why they do horribly, they are quick to tell you that they hate English, or math, or biology, or their horrible, boring, cranky, lame, kid-hating teacher who, for no reason whatsoever (since *they* never did anything wrong), hates them and treats them unfairly. Since they have no specific goal that they are working toward, they let any obstacle block their way because that's as far as they can see.

It isn't that way with students who have clear-cut goals because they approach things differently. Instead of getting bogged down in whether or not she likes the teacher, or subject, or class, the goal-oriented student focuses on the task at hand and doesn't let these other factors distract her. Maybe she thinks the subject is boring, or the teacher is boring, or mean, or stupid, or whatever. It just doesn't matter to her because all of these things are beside the point. The goal-oriented student knows that even after the class is left behind, the grade remains. So she keeps her mind on the goal of getting the A and moves on, whether she likes the situation or not.

The View From Both Sides of the Fence

I have to admit that I learned this idea the hard way. Throughout high school, I was the classic complainer. I would happily tell anyone how dumb my classes were, not to mention the stupidity of the fact that I had to spend so much time dealing with things that I was never going to use in my life, ever. Needless to say, I was a terrible student, and my report cards reflected the fact. (I didn't get a single A, got maybe one or two B's, and the rest of my grades were C's, D's, and F's.)

When I graduated, I had no direction and no intention of getting anywhere near a college. But after eight years of dead end jobs, frustration, and feeling like a total loser, I finally decided to go back to school. Desperately intent on making up for lost time, I had a different attitude altogether. I also had a definite goal—I was determined to get straight A's. It took three semesters to do it, but once I did, I continued to get straight A's the rest of the way. Talk about changing identity. One of the biggest factors in being able to make such a leap in results was realizing that my feelings about the class or teacher or whatever had nothing to do with my performance or my determination to achieve my goal. And believe me, I had plenty of classes I absolutely hated. Goals help you get past the distractions.

Goals Help to Keep You Motivated

Look, just because you have a specific direction you are heading in and you have a workable plan to achieve it, doesn't mean that every step of the way is going to be easy. Or fun. Without goals, people get sidetracked easily whenever their initial inspiration wears off (and it always does.) You know from anything you've worked on, whether it was a sport, musical activity, or whatever you might have done, that sometimes it's not as fun or exciting as other times. This is natural, so you basically have two choices: quit or go on. People without specific goals generally quit and move from whim to whim, never sticking with anything and wondering why they're unhappy. (They also spend a lot of time putting down other people who are accomplishing something.)

But people with specific goals find that having a definite direction to move in allows them to focus on the ultimate result and push through the difficult times, the times when they just don't want to do it (whatever it is). By seeing the big picture and the ultimate reward, you can keep your excitement level higher and take greater steps toward your goal. The great thing about this is that every little victory or accomplishment along the way fuels you with more excitement, which in turn drives you to accomplish more. It's called an upward spiral of achievement, and it feels incredible.

Goals Can Make Hard Work Fun

When you have a specific goal you are working on, it makes working hard not only easier, but believe it or not, it can make it fun. Like I said before, accomplishing things is much more fun than sitting around complaining about being bored or whatever. Pursuing a goal makes you *want* to excel, which lets you tap resources that you might not believe you had, or wouldn't have used, if you hadn't been focusing on your goal. Again, there's no hocus-pocus magic wand here. It's not that goals somehow produce resources or abilities you don't already have; it's that they provide the direction and motivation needed to bring into play resources and abilities that you do possess but aren't using. Years back, I had an experience that perfectly illustrated the truth of this last point.

While hiking a trail one day in a park just north of San Francisco, I found a hilltop that overlooked the ocean and had a great view of the hills in the east. It was the highest point in the park and it struck me as the perfect spot to watch a sunrise. The only problem was that I would have to start two hours before dawn if I went the way I usually did. The trail down to the trailhead was much shorter than the approach trail, but it was incredibly steep. Normally, I would never have considered going up that way because it seemed way too difficult. When I decided to reach the peak before sunrise, however, things changed.

Now I had a specific goal, and I was excited about accomplishing it. Returning to the park the next weekend, I was determined to beat the sun, which was to rise at 5:49 that day. It was 5:15 when I arrived, so I had thirty-four minutes to make the two-mile climb up the peak. That hill was a monster, but now that I had my goal, I was driven to succeed—I *had* to reach the peak before the sun broke the horizon. Instead of dreading such an exhausting endeavor, I was psyched and having a blast.

Even though my legs were killing me and I was gasping for air, the idea of succeeding felt so good that it overpowered any idea of stopping or slowing down. Instead, I just powered up that trail. I made it with four minutes to spare, and the feeling of victory was indescribable. I had performed at a level *far* beyond any that I had ever experienced before.

What was it that allowed me to perform at this higher level? If I were just hiking up this trail, I wouldn't have worked nearly as hard. But because I had a specific goal of beating the sunrise, it gave me the focus and determination to achieve results beyond what I was normally accustomed to producing. It opened a channel into deeper resources that I had never used before, resources that I didn't even know I possessed. Also, it made working hard exciting and more fun than I thought was possible.

Deep within man dwell those slumbering powers;
powers that would astonish him,
that he never dreamed of possessing;
forces that would revolutionize his life
if aroused and put into action.
—*Orison Swett Marden*

The Size of the Goal is Not the Important Thing

We tend to think that only large-scale accomplishments or big situations can be major victories. This isn't true. The preceding example had a major impact on me, but it wasn't a major incident in the big picture. After all, it *was* just a hike, however rigorous. But the lesson it taught cut deep. Now, when I get in a situation where I don't think I can do something, whether big or small, I recall that race to beat the sunrise. I know that I have the ability within me, if I will only make up my mind to use it and follow through. So remember, it's not the size of the goal that you set, it's your desire to set it and achieve it. Once you do, you can use it to reinforce your confidence and further condition your belief that you *are* successful. Also, success is success. If you can do it in one area, it's a good bet that you can do it in others as well, because you are using the same traits. That's the beauty of the elements of achievement—they are point and shoot. Wherever you aim them, you get better results.

Goals Help You Break Out of Your Comfort Zone

Another important point illustrated in the hiking example is the idea of reaching for something beyond what you think you can do. Generally, we all like to work within a certain set of limits, a place that is familiar and doesn't present us with any surprises. This place is known as the "comfort zone," and we all have one, although some people have an easier time getting beyond theirs. (Don't let the name fool you. The comfort zone isn't always a positive place because it often holds us back from new experiences and chances to grow.) When something comes up that is beyond our comfort zone, we tend to fear it, or reject it, or jump to conclusions as to why it won't work, or why it's impossible, or stupid, or whatever.

Many students have comfort zones that are quite rigid, and it is often difficult to get them to see past them. These are the kids who are quick to insist (often with great vehemence) that they can't write very well, that they can't take tests, that they are going to do poorly on certain assignments because they just aren't good at that stuff, etc. Of course, these attitudes come from limiting beliefs and can be overcome by using the techniques laid out in the chapter on beliefs. One of the hardest things to do, however, is to get these students to even attempt to change because the very idea of doing something different, of producing new results in their area of weakness, goes beyond their comfort zone. And because of this, they refuse to take any action at all. Hey, not all prisons have bars.

In situations where you become fenced in by your comfort zone, a goal can be a very effective means of pulling you through—if you make sure that it is something that goes beyond what you normally would attempt to do. This is what happened in my hiking example. I set a goal that was far beyond my comfort zone, far beyond what I normally would have attempted or what I thought I could do. By accomplishing it, I discovered not only how limiting my comfort zone was, but also just how possible it was to overcome it when the need arose.

The Momentum Goals Provide Helps You Persevere

When you get going on a goal, you start to build up momentum and the whole process becomes easier. After all, isn't getting started the hardest part of any project? Much of the reason for this is that we frequently aren't sure of where we are going, so we drag our feet. With a clear goal, we can get excited because the uncertainty has been removed and we don't have any doubts about what we are going after.

Also, this momentum is valuable in helping you to keep going when things get difficult or start going wrong. As I said earlier, many people, since they don't have their goals in order, give up their pursuit of something when things start to get difficult. Instead of sticking it out, they run away and begin to chase after something else that looks easier. What they fail to realize is that once the novelty wears off, anything worth pursuing is going to involve periods where things get tough.

It's not that I'm so smart, it's just that I stay with problems longer.
—Albert Einstein

Can you imagine a great athlete, or musician, or scientist, or business person who didn't have the perseverance to push through the tough times? I can't either, because such a person doesn't exist. Every field or pursuit has its difficulties, and in every field, there are those who succeed and those who quit. It's the person with the clearly defined goal that becomes successful, because the goal provides a constant target to aim for. The momentum he or she builds up as the pursuit gets under way helps push barriers aside.

This is the role goals play in the achievement process: **Know exactly what you are going for**, consistently see yourself as having already accomplished it, fully expect that you will do so, and feel that way.

Give me a stock clerk with a goal
and I'll give you a man who will make history.
Give me a man with no goals, and I'll give you a stock clerk.
—J. C. Penny

Guidelines for Setting Goals

When it comes to pursuing your goals, there are a few guidelines to help you get the most out of your effort. The first one is for long-term goals. Certainly, for something short-term or a one-timer like my hill-climbing goal, this isn't necessary.

One: Write down your goals and goal plans in detail

For different reasons, people usually want to skip this part. Of course, there is the resistance that many students generally have to writing *anything* down. But beyond that, there seems to be the idea that merely figuring out this stuff mentally will work just as well. It won't. First of all, by being unwilling to commit your goals to writing, you are sending a message to your mind that you are not truly serious about accomplishing them. Before you object to this idea, consider the possible reasons for not writing down your goals.

Can you honestly say that your reasons for not writing them down are not grounded in either laziness or fear? By failing to write your goals down, you will be missing out on two advantages that will prove highly beneficial to your success: clarity and permanence.

By writing down your goals and plans, you begin to see more clearly what needs to be done in order for you to be successful. When you limit your goals to mental figuring, you are bound to leave out important details. When you write them down and stand back from them, you can see them for what they are, not what you think they are.

Have you ever taken notes during a class and later had trouble figuring out what they were about? What happened was that when you were taking notes, you were filling in the details, or context, in your head, so what you wrote made perfect sense. Later, when the details were pushed aside by whatever you had to do next period or something else that you got involved in, the context of the notes was lost, so they weren't as clear anymore.

It's the same with your goals. You are inclined to forget details that seemed so clear when you initially worked out your ideas. By writing them down, you not only are able to work out important details, but you also get a better picture of what you are working toward. When something is only in your mind, it tends to shift as time goes on. When your goals are only mental, they will lose their clarity. As situations arise and you naturally start making adjustments to adapt, you may find yourself working toward something quite different than your original goal. This "something different" can easily turn out to be much less than you were initially going for. You can wind up doing the same amount of work and get far less than what you could have gotten if you hadn't lost sight of your original goal.

Of course, having mental goals is better than having no goals at all, but if you are serious about accomplishing what you originally set out to do, be smart and write down what you are going after. Then, you can review your goal and get fresh inspiration and motivation, especially when things get difficult. And they will get difficult at some point.

As soon as you realize the goal that you want to pursue, begin writing a preliminary plan for achieving it. Again, it's easy to see why you might want to resist this, but it really is in your best interest to do it anyway. A written plan does two things for you. It makes your goal that much more real to your mind when you have some sort of plan to achieve it, and it helps you to organize your resources and strategies in a way that you can review periodically. Also, writing things down forces you to concentrate more on what you are doing, and it also quickly shows you how vague your ideas can be.

Often, people think that they know just what they are after, but when they try to write their goals and plans down, they realize that they can't get a clear handle on what they are doing. It's a very efficient test: If you can't write it down in a clear manner, you haven't thought it through enough. This does not mean that you need to have every detail of your plan firmly in place before you begin, but it does mean that you need to know what you are going after. When writing your plan, consider these questions regarding your goal:

+What will you need to achieve your goal?
+What resources do you have to help you?
+Who can you find to help you achieve your goal?
+Who is already getting the results that you want?
+How much time will you need daily to work on your goal?
+What is standing in the way of your success?
+How can you remove these obstacles?
+What skills will you need in order to achieve your goal?
+What characteristics will you need?

When it comes to finding help, think of friends, family, teachers, and administrators. You might feel that teachers and administrators would be too busy, or not want to help you. For the most part, this isn't true. If a teacher or administrator sees a student who is determined to succeed, they will usually bend over backwards to help that student. Even if you haven't had the best relationship with them up to this point, if they see you are sincere and want to make things better, they will certainly help you. Most people, even teachers and administrators, would rather have positive interactions with you than negative ones. It just makes things so much easier.

As for people you know who are getting the kind of results you want, what are they doing to get these results, and how can you do the same? This concept is called modeling and it is extremely valuable. If you can, take the effort to find some models because you will save a lot of time and effort in the long run. Again, you might think that someone would not be willing to help you, but you would be surprised. If you approach someone sincerely with the idea of modeling him or her, they will generally be glad to help you. Think about it. You are telling them that you want to be like them. People love to share their success with other people. It gives them validation that they are successful.

The last two bullets involve the type of person you need to be in order to get the job done. This, of course, has everything to do with identity. (By now, I'm sure you are seeing how all of this stuff works together.)

Write the answers down. It doesn't have to include every question here, but the more details you can come up with, the better off you will be. The clearer the picture your mind can grab on to, the more compelled it will be to move you in the direction of your goal.

Of course, writing down your goals does not mean that you are locked into them if you realize that changes in your plan are necessary. Sometimes, as you move along in your pursuit, you see things that you didn't consider initially. Fine. Make the necessary adjustments and keep on working.

Two: State your goal in the positive

You don't want goals that merely move you away from negative situations, but ones that move you toward positive ones. Of course, getting away from negative situations is a good start, but it's not the place to stop. Nor will it take you as far as you ultimately want to go. For example, say you set a goal of no longer failing math. What you have here is a goal stating what you don't want—to fail math. It's not a bad idea, not failing math, but it has its problems as a goal. For one thing, you wouldn't want to limit yourself to just passing math if, using the same amount of effort, you could do much better by being more focused and positive.

The motivation you have for achieving a goal comes in part from the excitement that is generated by the goal itself. Which accomplishment do you think would make you happier and more excited—getting a D in a subject you had previously failed, or getting an A or B? Which goal do you think is going to drive you toward using resources that you don't normally use? And yes, it *is* possible to make large leaps in progress like going from F's to A's. Remember Matt? (See Chapter Two.)

Also, if you have a goal that is stated in the negative, you are spending much of your time focusing on what you don't want. For instance, say that you design a goal that is stated, "I will no longer procrastinate when it comes time to do my homework." As you will learn in the upcoming chapter on focus, you tend to get what you pay attention to. Even though you don't want to procrastinate any longer, your attention, as dictated by the language of your goal, is still on procrastination. So it is better to state your goal in the positive: "I will do my assignments as soon as I get home from school." (Or whatever your goal is.) Stated this way, you are putting your attention on what you want, instead of on what you don't want. As another example, instead of stating your goal, "I will not get angry whenever such and such happens," state it in the positive: "I will stay calm whenever such and such happens." It seems like a small difference, but with the first, your mind is still focusing on anger, the thing you want to get rid of, while in the second, your mind is focusing on staying calm, the thing you want. This is the better way to go because it allows all parts of your mind to move in the same direction, thereby improving your prospects of succeeding.

Three: Make sure your goal is something you can control

You want to be sure that what you are after is something that is within *your* control. It shouldn't be dependent on someone else in order for it to be accomplished. For example, goals like, "my friends won't bother me when it is time to study," or, "my algebra teacher will not be so mean to me," are not within your control because other people have to do certain things in order for your goal to be accomplished. You only want to have to pay attention to and be responsible for your performance, not someone else's. These goals can be reworded so that they will accomplish the same objective, but with you as the focus. For example, "I will stay focused when it is time to study" accomplishes the same objective as, "my friends won't bother me when it's time to study," but it puts you in control. "I will stay out of my algebra teacher's face" puts you in control of your objective. Of course, there's no guarantee that your algebra teacher won't be mean to you, but at least *you* are behaving properly. Having a cranky algebra teacher may just be your lot in life, as it was mine. But if your goal puts you in control of obtaining your objective, at least you won't be putting yourself in the line of fire as often. You just get you're A and move on.

Four: Be able to tell when you have reached your goal

This is such an important point because you need to know when you have been successful. It sounds funny, but often, people set goals that are so vague that they never appreciate the progress they make. This is why you don't want to set goals such as, "I will be a better student," or, "I will work harder in Spanish." How will you know when you are getting "better" or working "harder," when you are doing "good" or "great," or when you are "improving"? All of these descriptions are too vague. You need to be specific in your goal in order to have clear evidence of your success. To be sure that you are doing this when you make your goals, just ask yourself the question: "How will I know when I have accomplished my goal?" If you can answer the question easily, then you know that your goal is specific enough. If not, reword it so that you can tell when you have succeeded.

Something that can all too easily happen when we are working on goals that are stated vaguely is that we lose sight of our achievements. This happens because when we do improve at something, we are inclined to take for granted what once was quite an accomplishment.

For example, several years back, I started running every day to get in shape. Initially, there was a certain hill that I always walked up because it was too hard to run up it. (Oh no, not another hill story!) One day, as I started out on my run, I was considering taking a shot at running up the hill, but I wasn't all that serious about it. When I got there, there was this guy who looked about twenty years older than I was, running toward the hill from another direction. So I said to myself, "If *he* runs up that thing, *I'm* going to do it, too." Well, he started up it, and I followed, using him as my motivation to make it. We were both running very, very slowly, but we kept on running. By the time I started to get close to the top, I thought I was going to fall over dead. Needless to say, I was proud of myself when I made it, because I had pushed myself hard and accomplished a specific goal that I had set for myself.

After a while, however, because I had improved in my running ability, it was no big deal for me to get to the top of that hill. But that doesn't diminish the victory I achieved that day. As with my other hill experience when I was hiking, I can use that experience as a confidence booster when I am confronted with a new situation where I need to dig deep. Because my goal was specific, I can look back on it for inspiration, knowing that since I succeeded then, I can succeed in the future. If I had only had vague goals about "getting better" at running, or "improving," or "running harder," it would have been much more difficult to draw on them for inspiration because I wouldn't have clear evidence that I had really succeeded at something.

Also, since it became a lot easier for me to get up that hill, doesn't that indicate that I was *not* working as hard? In a sense, it does indicate that. Since I was in better condition, I didn't have to work as hard to get the same results. If I had been working with a vague goal such as, "I will work harder at my running," I could have easily begun to feel like I was failing, when in fact, it is only because I was improving that I didn't have to work as hard. Or, I would have only felt that I was being successful when I was accomplishing something as difficult as getting up that hill the first time, which is not something that I would be able to manufacture every day. With specific goals you can keep close tabs on your progress, but with vague goals, you can lose sight of what you are accomplishing and feel like you are going backward when you are actually moving forward.

Five: Have a timeline for your goal

Nobody seems to like this one. I guess it's natural to be a little hesitant when it comes to doing something like this because it seems like we're putting undue pressure on ourselves. But this isn't the way we should approach the idea. For one thing, we ultimately work better, or at least a little harder, when there is some kind of deadline motivating us. I know that I have a tendency to drift a little when the completion of a project or task doesn't have a back end to it. I have also found that I can get a lot more out of myself, even in little things, when I give myself a timeline.

For example, when I was a classroom teacher, grading papers was not my favorite activity, but it's something that I had to do. What I used to do was complain to myself about it and put it off whenever possible. (Of course, this sounds just like the students' reaction to doing the assignments in the first place.) By learning to apply the same stuff that I am teaching you here, I changed my approach. When I had to grade a stack of papers, I looked at the clock and told myself that these papers would be finished by whatever o'clock. It sounds simple, but it really did make a huge difference in the amount of work I got done.

Once, during summer school, I got a stack of tests that would have taken well over an hour if I hadn't put any deadline on the task. I looked at the clock and saw that I had thirty-five minutes before the end of the class. The students were working on the essay section of the test, so without even thinking about it, I told myself that I'd finish grading the papers before the end of class. It didn't seem like nearly enough time, given the normal pace at which I graded papers, but I attacked the pile and never let up, finishing with two or three minutes to spare.

There are important points to be learned from this seemingly insignificant incident. I chose this example *because* it was a little thing, the kind you can find any day of the week. You do not need to find major, earthshaking events to put these principles into action. Being consistent in the small stuff, as any successful person will tell you, is far more important to your overall success than overlooking the details while you search for dramatic challenges.

Putting a timeline on my goal allowed me to reach down and come up with a level of effort that I didn't normally use when grading papers. This is significant because, like I said, I *really* didn't like grading papers. By knocking them out in such a short span, I realized again that whether or not I enjoyed doing the task had nothing to do with the level of energy I put into it. This is such a key point that I am tempted to say that it might be the most important thing you could learn at this point in your efforts. So let me say it again: Whether or not you like doing something (or think it is boring) should have no bearing on the amount of effort you put into it, if it is important to your success and helps you achieve your goals.

But you know what? Something interesting happened when I put a timeline on the goal. Instead of griping about having to grade the papers, my focus went to whether I could get them done in time. I was in the middle of a challenge and it became a competition. So instead of having a bad time, I was having a lot of fun doing something I'd rather not have to do at all.

But what if I hadn't finished in time? After all, the only reason I had picked that timeline was because it was what was left of the period. I didn't stop to think whether I could do it. (Which is a good thing because if I had, I probably wouldn't have gone through with it, limiting beliefs being what they are.)

I am looking for a lot of men who have an infinite capacity to not know what can't be done.
—Henry Ford

Ultimately, it wouldn't have made much difference because the timeline wasn't the most important thing. Whether or not you achieve your goal within the timeline you set, you will work much better and get more done than if you hadn't set one at all. Obviously, when you are working on goals that take more planning and consideration, you don't want to just set any old timeline, thinking, "hey, if I make it, ok; if I don't, fine." You want to sincerely work to get done under the wire. It's best to think about how long it would take you to do the task and then set a timeline which is shorter than you thought it would take. That way, you will be pushed to work harder than you would have ordinarily. Just make sure you understand that if you work hard and don't meet your timeline, you shouldn't feel like you failed; you just needed more time to accomplish your goal. (For example, I missed the first timeline for the completion of this book, so I made a new one and moved on. I missed that one too, and two more after that. Finally, here it is, under the wire for the fifth one.) Timelines are important, but you needn't be tied to them to the point of beating yourself up about it. They are there to guide and motivate you, not to punish you. (Of course, due dates for assignments are a different story altogether, right?)

Six: Begin, even if you aren't sure how to proceed
Although I talked about writing out your goals and plans in detail, there's no reason for you to expect to have all of your plans figured out before you start. If you do have a clear idea of how to go about what you are after, fine. But if it were necessary to have everything ready to go before you started, many successful people would not have been able to accomplish much of what they have done. There have been many cases where the only thing that was clear at the beginning was the strong desire to achieve their particular goal. Ultimately, that desire is the only

thing that's necessary in order to get started. *Your willingness to go after it is by far the most important factor in achieving your goal.* There are people who will not start anything until they have everything figured out. The sad thing is that they wind up never getting to that point, so they never take action. You don't want to be one of these people, do you?

Take the first step in faith.
You don't have to see the whole staircase, just take the first step.
—Martin Luther King

If there is something that you really want to pursue but don't know how to go about it, don't let that stop you. Just start working toward it in any way that you can. If you are really serious about achieving it, what you will see happen is that as you begin pursuing your goal, ideas and assistance will become available to you. (One of the main reasons why this happens is something called your RAS, which is discussed in detail in the next chapter.) So don't limit your goals to what you think *might* be possible or what you think you *might* be able to do. These limiting beliefs do not serve you well; they are not your friends. If you want something, go after it, regardless of whether or not you know exactly how to get it. The desire to achieve something goes a long way toward opening doors you aren't even aware of when you get started.

Whatever you can do, or dream you can—begin it.
Boldness has genius, power, and magic in it.
—Johann Wolfgang Goethe

The Higher You Aim, the Farther You Fly

I've already mentioned that nobody succeeds without failing a lot along the way. This is true, but it is also true that we can often see successes as failures because we didn't get 100% of what we were going after. This can be a problem for some people, causing them to pull back when it comes to going after goals. But, as usual, it's all a matter of how we look at things, as we can see in the following illustration.

John and Jane have both been getting D's in their math class and have decided they needed to improve. John set a goal of getting a C and Jane set a goal of getting an A. At the end of the semester, John got his C and Jane got a B. Which student was more successful?

You could say that John was more successful because he set a goal and achieved it, while Jane set a goal and failed to achieve it. But it can also be pointed out that Jane's "failure" brought her twice as much improvement than John's "success" brought him.

You might say that John would have been better off if he had aimed for an A like Jane did, and there is something to this. But it's fine to take small steps if it helps you gain confidence. Once you see that you *can* do what you set out to do, then by all means, start aiming higher. The higher you aim, the farther you fly. Even if you don't make it 100%, you will still make more progress than if you only take small steps all the time.

In the long run, men hit only what they aim at.
Therefore, they had better aim at something high.
—Henry David Thoreau

What You Become is More Important than What You Get

Of course, just setting goals in and of itself will not get the job done. After all, having a road map might tell you how to get where you are going, but it isn't going to drive the car. You are still going to have to do the work in order to make your goals become reality. But having the goals is a critical step in achieving your dreams.

Hopefully, you now have a better understanding of why goals are such an important element when it comes to your success. Before moving on, however, I want to raise a point that often gets lost in all of the emphasis on goals.

If you have come this far, you are most likely serious about succeeding. This being the case, you will be setting and achieving many goals, now and in the future. But there is one point you should understand if you want to be truly successful: The kind of person you become because of your goals is more important than the goals themselves.

Accomplishing a lot of goals, in and of itself, is no guarantee of that you are going to be happy. In other words, there are many supposedly "successful" people living lives filled with frustration and unhappiness. Does this mean that you can't be successful and happy at the same time? Of course not. It simply means that it is important to think about what you are going after, why you are going after it, and what kind of person you will become in the process.

For example, someone who uses this knowledge to become a successful lawyer because that is what is expected of them, even though they never wanted to be a lawyer, is not going to be successful, even if they wind up becoming the head partner of the biggest law firm in town. Why? Because they have followed somebody else's dreams, and even though they have all the outward trappings of success, they are going to have a difficult time feeling good about it if it isn't what they really wanted.

There are more elements to success than making a lot of money or having a prestigious career. Although there is nothing wrong with wanting these things, you need to give attention to other aspects of your life as well, aspects that many people seem to forget about when they think of what it means to be a success. For instance, would you want to be a rich and famous person who suffered from chronic ulcers and generally wretched health? How about a rich and famous person who went through one divorce after another, or who couldn't get along with his or her family or people in general and had no peace of mind whatsoever? No one would pick these types of situations if they had the choice. Regardless of what some people will try and tell you, you do have a choice. Success doesn't have to mean making tons of enemies and sacrificing other aspects of your life in order to achieve your goals.

A balanced life pays proper attention to your material, social, spiritual, and health concerns. Your goals, far from being ends in themselves, are most valuable when they serve as the means to aid you in acquiring this balanced life, which is far more fulfilling, and therefore, successful, than just getting stuff and being hated by everybody you clobbered on the way up the ladder. So pay attention to the kinds of goals you set because they will determine the direction in which you travel. Despite what many people would have you believe, the more you help other people, the more you yourself are helped.

Of course, once you determine your goals, you should program them into your mind daily by visualizing what your life will be like and how you will feel when you have accomplished them. Get excited about them, certainly. After all, they *are* going to change your life.

Twenty years from now you will be more disappointed by the things that you didn't do than by the ones you did do. So throw off the bowlines. Sail away from the safe harbor. Catch the trade winds in your sails. Explore. Dream. Discover.
—*Mark Twain*

The most important key to achieving great success is to decide upon your goal and launch. Get started, take action, move!
—*John Wooden*

The world makes way for the man who knows where he is going.
—*Ralph Waldo Emerson*

Chapter Five

Focus—
Hey, Look at That

Tell me what you pay attention to, and I will tell you who you are.
—Jose Ortega y Gasset

Yes, you should be excited about your goals, since they do have the power to dramatically change the quality of your life. But you don't want your life to consist only of possible future successes because that is a sure way of missing out on the present, the only part of life that you actually get to walk around in.

Many people spend the majority of their time either worrying about the future or feeling guilty about the past. You definitely want to watch out for these twin traps of misery. Successful people, while mindful of the past and future, live in the present. Again, what you become through accomplishing your goals is far more important than the goals themselves. In other words, the process is just as important as the results you get from it. If you want to find some truly sad people, look no further than those who have ignored this fact. There they are, wondering what to do now after they have accomplished everything they set out to do, often after years of hard work and sacrifice, and they *still* don't feel fulfilled because they ignored the present while always looking to the future. What they didn't realize is that the future never gets here, so when they accomplished their goals they were left asking themselves, "is this all there is?" There they were, wondering why they felt so empty. Not a situation you want to be in, is it?

So, if you aren't particularly interested in being miserable today while waiting for tomorrow's happiness (which never seems to get here), you will want to pay close attention to the next two chapters because they deal with the keys to getting the most out of *right now:* focus and state of mind.

> *Yesterday is history, tomorrow a mystery;*
> *today is a gift, which is why it's called the present.*
> —*Babatunde Olatunji*

Simple Doesn't Mean Easy

The biggest problem with focus and state is not that they are so complicated, but that they are so simple. Some people initially have difficulty believing that such simple concepts can have such an enormous impact on their lives. Part of this is because they are confusing "simple" with "easy." Even though we interchange them all the time, they really are different.

Have you ever walked a tightrope? It's really quite simple. Here's how you do it: place one foot in front of the other on the rope. Repeat until you reach the other end. Or how about saying the alphabet backwards? Here's how you do it: start at Z and go in reverse order until you get to A. In each case, what could be simpler?

But not so easy, huh? I'm putting special emphasis on this distinction because the concepts and techniques you are learning here *are* simple, but they may not be easy to do at first. That's ok—it's why they invented practice. You don't want to fall into the trap of dismissing something because it seems too simple.

You Can't Focus on Everything

Focus is simply what you are paying attention to at any given moment. It doesn't sound like a big deal, but the effect it has on your everyday life is enormous. In fact, ultimately, the quality of your experience on a day-to-day basis (or more accurately, on a minute-by-minute basis) is directly tied to your focus.

This one's going to take some explaining, so here we go. Of all of the things going on around you, what are you aware of right now as you read this? Maybe you are aware of the words on the page, but are you aware of the weight of the book in your hand? How about the temperature in the room? Is it too hot, too cold, just right? Is there any noise in the room—other people talking, clock ticking, window rattling, heater or air-conditioner noise, refrigerator noise, traffic outside? What about the brightness or dimness of the light, the color of the walls, the texture of the rug or the surface of the floor, the shape of the tiles on the ceiling? Are there any smells you hadn't noticed? Food cooking, someone's perfume or cologne? How does your back feel sitting in that hard chair? Are your legs stiff from running, or basketball practice yesterday? On and on it goes.

You see, your conscious mind doesn't pay attention to everything that is happening around you. It can't, since to do so would overwhelm you because there's just too much happening at any one instant. Now, if your conscious mind can't pay attention to all of the things going on around you, do you think it can pay attention to everything happening *within* you—your emotions, fears, dreams, goals, regrets, likes, dislikes, hopes, and so on? Obviously, it cannot. You know from your own experience that in order to pay close attention to one thing, whether a feeling, thought, or outward event, you have to stop paying attention to something else. What you are doing when you divert your attention in this way is shifting your focus. Simple, sure, but it is almost impossible to overestimate how important it is to be able to have some control over it.

You Do Choose Your Focus, So What Will You Choose?

Since there's too much going on around you and within you for you to deal with at one time, you have to choose, or focus on, a particular portion. So how do you decide what you are going to focus on? If you're like most people, you don't even think about it and just follow your habitual patterns of focus. Of course, if your habitual patterns are generally negative, your focus isn't serving you very well, is it?

A man is what he thinks about all day long.
—Ralph Waldo Emerson

For illustrative purposes, let's look at an average school day from the point of view of someone who has a negative focus: "Look, as a general premise, school sucks. Period. After all, the teachers are the worst. They're only concerned with how they can ruin my day. I mean, what are they *doing* up there? They lecture me into a coma with a constant, never-ending stream of useless information that has *nothing* to do with real life, right? Then, when they're done with that, they give me some impossible test, or stupid writing assignment that has nothing to do with anything *I* care about. And if I *were* to bother writing about something that I *did* care about, they're only going to flunk me anyway. Why do I have to bother with this stuff? Science, math, history . . . what's it got to do with *my* life? And English? Hey, I can already *speak* the language. Why do I have to keep learning about it?

"And, as if the teachers weren't bad enough, I have to put up with all of these nerds that insist on doing whatever they can do to make me look bad—these goody-goodies with their raised hands and right answers and everything turned in on time. Do they have a *life* or what? And please, don't even talk to me about the horror that is PE, or the food in the cafeteria. Just wake me when this nightmare is over, and let me know when I can get *on* with my life!"

We are Trained to See a Negative Focus

I wish I could say that the above portrayal is an exaggeration, but in my experience, it is all too common. Easy, too. With such an outlook, a student can blame everything on someone else, right? Of course, I can't fault a student too much for having such a focus. After all, it's easy to adopt such an outlook because we are trained to focus on the negative, aren't we? Look at the evening news: "This is Peter Jennings with today's menu of fresh catastrophe. You know the tune, so sing along. Our specials are:

Twelve wars a raging
eleven bombers bombing
ten crooks in Congress
nine brokers cheating
eight treaties broken
seven scandals brewing
six spies a singing
five
failed
banks
four forests cut
three drug lords
two oil spills
and the stock market just took a dive!"

Every day thousands of planes take off without a hitch, but if one crashes, it's film at eleven. Sure, no news is good news, but it's equally true that good news is no news. It's the negative that gets our attention. After a steady diet of it day in and day out, it doesn't take long to figure that this is just the way it is and everything surely must suck because that's all we ever hear about—things that suck.

Just Another Rotten Day Made to Order

But just because a negative focus is easy to have, that doesn't necessarily mean you want one. In fact, think about the price you pay for having one. What if you were like the student with the negative focus described above? What kind of experience would you be likely to have on a daily basis? Each day, you get to school expecting everything about it to suck. And of course, you are right. It does suck.

This is the main point concerning focus, why it is essential to understand the key role it plays in your life: In general, *you get what you focus on.* In other words, if you go looking for it, you're probably going to find it. You want to see everything in shades of gray? Fine. Gray it is. You want every class to be boring? Boring they will be. You need a reason why this assignment is stupid? No problem; your mind will give you three or four reasons without breaking a sweat. Are your classmates jerks? Well, hell, *look* at them! That one acts like this, this one acts like that, and that group over there is so pathetic that once again you are afraid you're going to have to run out of the room screaming just to keep from throwing a chair at them. Hey, you want it, you got it. If you focus on it, that's what you will see.

> *What we see depends mainly on what we look for.*
> —*Sir John Lubbock*

> *If you look for the bad in people,*
> *expecting to find it, you surely will.*
> —*Abraham Lincoln*

The Return of the "Reality" Demons

Is this negative focus your only option? I wish I could say it was obvious that it isn't, but a positive focus is often seen as one that is "not being realistic." I've heard this over and over, but the idea comes from a misunderstanding of what a positive focus actually is. So let's clear that up.

Having a positive focus does not mean telling yourself that everything is just exactly perfect. "Jeez, I had it all wrong! All of my classmates are great, all of my classes are greater, and all of my teachers are the greatest. I wish we could do this school thing twelve hours a day. And if we *must* have weekends off, couldn't we at least have twice as much homework?" *That* is certainly not being realistic. But it's also not at all what I am talking about here. Learning to shift your focus from negative to positive is about figuring out how you can turn a situation to your advantage instead of whining about it. Instead of continually resisting everything that comes your way by saying it's boring or stupid, ask yourself how you can benefit from it. It's simply the difference between asking, "How can I get out of this?" and, "What can I get out of this?" What's so unrealistic about that?

When we looked at beliefs, I said that it didn't matter whether the belief was accurate or not. If you believed it, you behaved as if it were true, so for you it was true. It's the same with focus. Whatever you choose to focus on becomes your reality because you are going to see the whole picture from that angle. It's not a question of whether you are right or wrong. Like the old saying about the glass being half empty or half full, the point isn't which one is the right answer. Both answers are equally correct. Don't let anybody tell you that you aren't being realistic if you aren't looking for the worst in everything. A negative focus isn't any more "realistic" than any other.

Although the world is full of suffering,
it is also full of the overcoming of it.
—*Helen Keller*

Stop Looking for What You Don't Want to Find

Often, when the subject of shifting one's focus comes up, some-one will ask whether it is wrong to pretend that things are differ-ent than they are. After all, if an assignment is stupid, it's stupid; if a teacher's boring, she's boring. The problem with this type of thinking is that things aren't automatically this way or that way. Of course, some people like to insist that they are only inter-ested in "objective reality" and protest against what I am saying here with statements like, "yeah, well, *I* live in the real world." It's funny how no two descriptions of that "real" world seem to match up, and that for some reason, whenever you ask these folks what that "real" world is like, it seems to bear an amazing resemblance to their particular worldview. The point beneath all of this talk about focus is simply this: a change in worldview changes the world viewed.

> *There is nothing either good or bad, but thinking makes it so.*
> *—William Shakespeare*

In all but the most extreme cases, we assign meaning to something and proceed from there. (We'll be dealing with this in detail in the next chapter.) Remember, since you can't con-sciously take in everything going on around you, or within you, you are always focusing on only a portion of the picture. But the great thing about this is that you do get to choose where your focus will be. So if you don't want to see the worst in every situation, the first and biggest step is to stop looking for it.

But just like I mentioned during our discussion on goals, you don't want to begin by telling yourself, "I will not focus on the negative," because by doing so, you will still be looking at the negative, since you are focusing on what you don't want, instead of what you do want. Instead, ask yourself, "what's positive about this situation?" If you are willing to persist beyond the first five seconds and the answer "nothing," your mind will provide you with legitimate answers and your focus will begin to shift.

Link Your Focus to Your Goals

To be sure, it's not always easy to change your focus just like that. If you've been working from a negative standpoint, you've had lots of time to program that pattern into your mind. It isn't going to change just because you wake up one day and say, "no more negative focus!" You're going to need to keep on top of your thought patterns, and as anyone who has ever attempted to do so will tell you, the mind is a slippery beast at best. Luckily, you now have tools to make your job easier.

So instead of trying to change your focus all by itself, link your focus to your goals. This makes your task easier because when you have your elements working together, it creates momentum. (The more energy you put into something, the more momentum you build up. The more momentum you build up, the more energy you get to work with. It's a great loop to be on.) It also shows you upfront whether or not your parts *are* working together. For example, as I said before, most students don't do as well as they could because when it comes to determining if they are going to do an assignment, or how much effort they will put into it, they get caught up in whether or not they like the assignment, or the subject, or the teacher, or whatever. If you have this problem, your focus is not being aimed in the right direction and isn't serving you well.

But your focus can serve you much better if you link it to a goal. For example, say you had the following goal to drive your focus: "I will do my assignments on time and ace them." Your positive focus and your goal can then work together to help you succeed. Instead of getting bogged down in whether you like the teacher or assignment, your focus is on your goal. So when you get an assignment, you jump right on it. If you are committed to achieving your goal, *it* becomes the most important part of the equation, not how you feel about geometry or vocabulary or whatever. By making this simple (but at first, not always easy) adjustment, you save an incredible amount of energy that you would normally use on resisting the assignment.

Focusing for Fun

Also, you can have a lot more fun, because you are succeeding in an area where you used to have trouble. It becomes like a contest you have with yourself. You can go from, "aaarrrgghh, I *hate* vocabulary; it's so booorrriinng. I'd rather poke sticks in my eye," to, "Ok, let's see how fast I can get this finished and still make sure I learn all the words." With the old way, you had lots of misery while the idea of doing the vocab was in the back of your head when you were procrastinating—and you still had to do it anyway. When you finally did it (if you did it) your heart wasn't in it, so you didn't do that well. Also, you probably did poorly on the test because you weren't prepared. That's no fun beforehand, no fun during, and no fun afterward. Not much of an opportunity to enjoy yourself in *this* recipe, is there?

But imagine having fun doing assignments you used to dread. It can happen, you know. When you get the assignment, you don't focus on the vocab, but on your goal. So instead of trying to find a way out of doing it, you go right after it because that's what you *do*. (Can you see how identity comes into this?) Where there was once pain in getting an assignment, you now get pleasure because you are anticipating a chance to achieve your goal and that feels good. While doing your vocab, you aren't doing it half-heartedly because you know your goal is to do your work to the best of your ability and ace the assignment. Again, accomplishing your goal is where your focus is, and you get pleasure from doing well on the assignment, not the assignment itself. By doing well on the assignment, you are naturally prepared for the test, so you ace that, which is also fun. Unlike before, you now can have fun beforehand, fun during, and fun afterward. And nowhere along the line did you have to talk yourself into liking vocabulary. Your success had nothing to do with liking vocabulary. (Obviously, this applies not only to vocabulary, but to all subjects and assignments.)

Only one thing has to change for us to know happiness in our lives: where we focus our attention.
—Greg Anderson

Your Brain's Standard Equipment for Focus
There is another important aspect concerning focus and your goals that we touched on in the last chapter. I said that if you really wanted to pursue a goal, you should just focus on it and get started on it right away, even if you didn't know how you

were going to accomplish it, because doors *will* open up for you, revealing needed information or resources to help you on your way.

Be bold and mighty forces will come to your aid.
—Basil King

Again, at any and every instant, there is far too much happening within you and around you for your conscious mind to cope with. Therefore, your mind focuses on only a narrow portion of this incoming data. Since most people don't pay attention to their focus, they are at the mercy of the habitual patterns that have been established by years of uncontrolled focusing.

But the question to be asked is: why do we focus on what we do? The answer lies in a part of the brain known as the reticular activating system, or RAS. While the RAS is quite complex from a neurological standpoint, for our purposes it is quite simple. One of the RAS's functions is to determine what we pay attention to or notice within the overwhelming flood of data we are continuously receiving. Essentially, here's how your RAS works as far as focus is concerned.

Let's say you just got some new shoes and are feeling good about them. You know what happens now, right? You begin seeing them all over the place—in commercials, in magazine ads, and especially on other people's feet. Why? Getting the shoes means that you are going to be focusing on them, since they are new (which makes them special). So you start seeing them everywhere. That's what your RAS does. It helps determine what your conscious mind pays attention to. The shoes were there the whole time, but your focus wasn't. You could have walked by ten pairs without noticing a single one. But now that they are a new part of your experience, you can spot them halfway down the hall out of the corner of your eye.

So it goes with your goals. When you focus on a goal, it becomes important to you and your RAS will alert you to anything connected to it within the flood of incoming data. What you see depends on where you put your focus. Even if you don't know how it will happen, if you are serious and keep focusing on your goal, you will find information and resources to help you achieve it. It's part of what your RAS does.

As much as I've gone on with the "there isn't any hocus-pocus magic wand" business, this is the part that really does sound like hocus-pocus. Whenever I talk with people about the RAS, the question comes up about whether it is just a coincidence that things connected to your goal start showing up. Some say it is, some say there's something else involved. I don't know if it's coincidence or not. All I know is that it *does* happen, and often. Ultimately, it doesn't matter one way or the other as far as results are concerned. If you insist that it is coincidence, that's fine with me. Just look at it as a way to make more coincidences happen so that you can take advantage of them.

Do not wait; the time will never be "just right."
Start where you stand, and work
with whatever tools you may have at your command,
and better tools will be found as you go along.
—Napoleon Hill

Aim Your RAS Toward the Positive

But be careful. Remember the "reality demons," those people who only see the downside of everything? You know now that this is because their focus is trained to find the bad in any situation or idea. You also know now that the whole time they are focusing on the negative, there are just as many positive aspects to be seen right in front of them, but they don't see them because their gaze is turned elsewhere (toward the negative.) This same principle applies to your goals. If you are focusing on reasons why something won't work, you *will* find them. But if you focus on reasons why you will accomplish something, you will find *them*, instead. Since you get what you focus on, focus on what you want to get, not on what you don't want.

Focus. It's a simple tool that can dramatically change the quality of your life on a daily basis. Use it properly and see the results it brings you.

To different minds, the same world is a hell, and a heaven.
—Ralph Waldo Emerson

Several tons of dirt must be moved to get an ounce of gold.
But you don't go into the mine looking for dirt.
You go in looking for gold.
—Andrew Carnegie

Chapter Six

State of Mind—
What Kind of Attitude is That?

*The greatest discovery of my generation is that a human being
can alter his life by altering his attitudes of mind.*
—*William James*

How are you feeling right now? Are you happy? Sad? Angry? Depressed, tired, excited, bored? A mix of some of the above? However you are feeling, it is the result of the state of mind you are in. State of mind (emotional state, mood, attitude—they're all names for the same element, which we will simply be calling state) is a key to your ability, as well as your inability, to perform at the levels necessary for you to be successful.

Think of your overall emotional experience as a radio dial, where each state is a "station." Negative states are down at the bottom, positive ones are up at the top, and neutral states are in the middle. At any moment during the day, we are tuned in to a particular station on the dial, whether positive, negative, or somewhere in between.

The way we deal with our emotional dial shapes our experience. Think of how many times have you heard someone say,

"It's all in your head." Well, in one sense, they're right. It *is* all in your head, because your behavior in any given situation is going to be influenced far more by your state than by what is happening on the outside. This might sound crazy at first, but take a look at your own life and you will see that it isn't that weird at all.

Haven't you had times where you were unable to do something because of the mood you were in, your energy level was too low, or you had an attitude? Haven't you also experienced times when, doing the same exact thing, you just cruised along, happy and energized, excited about what you were doing and knowing you would succeed without any problem?

What was different? It wasn't your ability to accomplish the task that differed dramatically. It was your state. What happens *inside* affects what happens *outside*, as much or more than the other way around. Where you are on the dial has a tremendous impact on how you react and what kind of results you get because of that reaction.

Your State Determines How You Will React

There's a classic illustration of how state affects our behavior: John was late for a meeting and was impatiently waiting for an elevator. When it finally arrived, it was packed. Instead of waiting for the next one, John decided to squeeze himself on, since he was behind schedule. As he was standing there on the way up to his floor, he felt something digging into his back. He didn't turn around to see who was jabbing him, but when they kept it up he knew they were getting back at him for forcing his way onto an already full elevator. As the elevator continued on its way, John began to get angry and started thinking about how rude people could be. He couldn't help that he was late. The more he thought about it, the angrier he got. As he reached his floor, he was determined to give the jerk who was jabbing him a piece of his mind because people who were that inconsiderate deserved whatever they got.

He got off the elevator, expecting to see his tormentor. Instead, John saw an old blind woman and the cane that had been pressing against his back. Now, instead of anger he immediately felt guilty for having had such thoughts about an old blind woman and quickly offered to help her off the elevator.

What was going on with John? In the space of a few seconds, he went from being outraged and wanting to tear someone's head off, to being overcome with guilt and rushing to give someone a hand. Nothing on the outside had changed in any way, but what he *thought* what was going on had changed dramatically. And it was what he thought was going on that determined his behavior, not the outside event. He thought *this* way, so he reacted *that* way. As I said in the chapter on belief, we don't react to what is happening; we react to what we *think* is happening. Always. (This may be the exception to the rule that every rule has an exception.)

We don't see things as they are, we see things as we are.
—Anais Nin

It's not what happens to you on the outside that makes you behave in a certain way, because when something happens on the outside there isn't just an automatic process in your mind that decides how you are going to behave. As with John in the elevator, your state determines how you are going to respond, and your state is affected by what you *think* is going on.

Think of your schoolwork. It's not the homework that you hate, and it's not the tests that you hate. If it were, then why do some people hate these things while other people don't mind them at all? (There isn't anything in the world that everyone thinks is good or everyone thinks is bad.) The way you behave depends on the *association*, or link, you make to the thing you are reacting to, what you are looking for from it.

If you are looking for constant pain and sorrow, sure algebra will give it to you. But if you are looking for a way to be successful at something, it will offer you that as well. Your state is determined by what you associate to the things that happen to you, not the things themselves. Take a test, for example; if you associate a bunch of negative baggage to it, it's the associations that you don't like, not the test.

So if you want to change the way you think about something, change the associations you link to it. Look at it and see the more positive things associated with it. Focus on the positive and your state will move toward the positive, focus on the negative and guess what? Remember what I've been saying over and over—your mind follows the directions you give it. That can be good news or bad news, depending on what you are consistently asking for.

If You Don't Like the Music—Change the Station

Most people just passively accept whatever state they are in, saying, "that's just the way I feel right now." They have no idea that they can change their state. But just because we develop habits when it comes to choosing certain reactions or states, does not change the fact that options do exist. Just like with the radio, so it is with your emotional dial—*if you don't like the music, change the station!* It can be done, and *you* can do it. Understanding and a little practice are all you need.

As I said in the last chapter, although goals are important for our future success, we don't want to forget about *right now* while we are planning for the future. Like focus, state is about right now. Your ability to effectively deal with your state right now does much to determine how well you do in the future because the road to the future is paved with a continuous series of right nows.

The premise of this book is that you, me, and everyone else all have within us abilities and resources that will aid us in achieving what we are striving for, *if* these capabilities are put into play. But we often don't tap them because of limiting beliefs and habitually negative states. If you are spending most of your time right now in unresourceful states, you are not going to be getting the best out of yourself in the future, either. If you want to consistently succeed, you've got learn to take control of, or manage, your state. This chapter is all about giving you tools that will aid you in doing so.

Posture is a Key to Your State

If there were three people in a room—one angry, one depressed, and one enthusiastic and happy—wouldn't you be able to tell which was which, even if they weren't saying anything? Can you tell when someone is upset without them telling you? How about when they are depressed? Haven't you asked a friend what was up, even though they insisted nothing was wrong? What is it that clues you in to what they are feeling?

A major indication is the way they are using their body. When someone is depressed they position their bodies in a certain way that lets you know how they are feeling. They hang their head and look at the floor, they droop their shoulders and sigh, right? But what about someone who is happy and enthusiastic? Have you ever seen them use their body as if they were depressed? Well, if not, why not? Why is it that you can generally tell if someone is happy or depressed, angry or whatever, even without them saying so?

One of the factors fundamentally determining state is our posture, or the way we position our bodies. I've said before that sometimes something is so simple that people don't want to believe it works. This is especially true when it comes to posture. Our posture plays a profound part in determining how we feel, but many people refuse to even experiment with it. After observing people with this in mind, I've become convinced that many people are content to feel rotten because there are substantial benefits to be gained from feeling that way.

Primary and Secondary Gain

I know it sounds crazy to say that someone would ever want to feel rotten by choice, but it's true. To make sense of it, we have to consider primary and secondary gain.

If you were taking a test, or writing an essay, or working on a science project, it seems reasonable to assume that you would want to get a good grade on it, doesn't it? Doing well on an assignment is the primary gain, and it's easy to understand because it's obvious. It's the upfront, logical answer to the question, "What's in it for me?"

But secondary gain isn't as obvious, and most of the time, people don't realize when they're pursuing it. For example, concerning physical well-being, it's safe to assume that everyone would want to feel as good as they could, right? Well, let's take a little quiz. Most people would prefer a state where:

a) they were filled with energy and enthusiasm
b) they had no energy and felt like they could barely get through the day

The obvious answer is a. But the correct answer is b.

It is easy to see the primary gain of choice a: having abundant energy is an invaluable aid, since rarely being tired or depressed or stressed out, you can do what needs to be done quickly, efficiently, and enthusiastically.

Well, who wants *that*?

Take a look around and it doesn't take long to notice that not too many people do, so why not? This is where secondary gain begins to make sense. When you have abundant energy and enthusiasm, you don't have any excuses for not getting the job done.

Imagine that. I think if there's one thing that most of us love above life itself, it's a good excuse for taking responsibility off of our shoulders. Whenever we can't get the job done, we look for an excuse. We all do it to some extent, sure, but what does it get us? We still fail, but with an excuse, we feel justified.

"Sure, I could have done it, but . . . " Of course, some excuses are better than others.

If your excuse is that you didn't study, or didn't pay attention, or were out with your friends, nobody is going to have much sympathy for your not getting the job done. Certainly, *you* know that you didn't put in the necessary effort. But if you are tired, or don't feel well, or are stressed out, there's more of a chance that you will be excused to some degree, even if it's only you who is doing the excusing. So if not feeling well or being tired all the time brings you the excuse you need to get you off the hook for not performing successfully, then that is the secondary gain of feeling rotten.

Body or Mind—Who's Following Who?

In any given situation, our actions are based on our desire to gain pleasure and avoid pain. If feeling rotten helps you get out of doing something that you thought you were going to have trouble with, and there is more pleasure in avoiding the task than in doing it, then you will gladly feel rotten in order to avoid the pain of having to do the task. But what if you are interested in succeeding and don't want to feel tired or stressed out because you find it getting in the way of your accomplishing your goals?

When we are tired, we are attacked by ideas we conquered long ago.
—Friedrich Nietzsche

After a while, feeling rotten begins to bring more pain than the (secondary) benefits it brings. What if you are sick and tired of feeling sick and tired? Changing your posture, or the way you use your body, is an incredibly effective way to change your state.

We don't usually think of the part that our bodies play in our moods and feelings, but we should. Say somebody is depressed. Do you think that the way they position their body has anything to do with the way they are feeling? Most people, when considering the connection between state and posture, just assume that a person's state is a product of the mind, and that their posture just reflects that state. In other words, if I appear depressed (i.e., slumped shoulders, sighing, looking at the floor, etc.) it is because I *am* depressed; my posture is only mirroring, or following, my state. But is it possible that using your body in a depressed manner can cause you to slip into a depression or deepen an already existing depression? Can you use your body in a way that makes you feel tired? Yes you can, and yes you do. You see, your posture doesn't only react to your state and follow along passively; it plays an active part.

Move *as if* You Have Energy, and You *Will* Have Energy
Mind and body work together to determine how we feel. If you habitually adopt a posture of depression, or tiredness, your mind will act upon the signals it receives from your body and respond accordingly. As I've been saying all along, your mind is similar to a computer in that it runs the program that you load into it. If, using your posture, you load a program that tells your mind that you feel tired, then your mind will accept the information and focus on reasons to be tired, thereby making you feel tired.

But what if you load in a program that has you feeling filled with energy? Since your posture helps determine your state, you can use this knowledge to your advantage. Let's assume that you are feeling tired but don't really want to. (I emphasize not wanting to because we've already looked at secondary gain and the benefits that a person can get from feeling rotten.) What can you do to feel better?

The easiest way to feel more energetic is to adopt a posture of energy and enthusiasm. That's right, just act *as if* you were filled with energy. Move your body as if you were totally pumped with energy. Breath deeply like you do when you are filled with energy. Behave like you would if you were filled with energy and enthusiasm. Do you know what will happen if you do this with sincerity? You will receive more energy and feel better. Just like that. I know it sounds too easy, but it *is* true.

If you want a quality, act as if you already had it.
—William James

Your Mind Acts on the Signals You Send It

It's not hard to understand how this concept of using your posture to switch gears on your state works. Why is it that you can recognize which person in the room is depressed or tired, and who is energized and enthused? Isn't it because people generally use similar postures for similar states? You know when someone is angry because they act angry. You know when someone is tired because they look tired. You know when someone is enthusiastic because they move like they are enthusiastic.

If the way others look, act, and move allows you to recognize their states, doesn't it make sense that you can recognize your own state by the way you look, act, and move? It sounds funny, but this is what your mind does when it receives the various signals from your body. If your body is sending signals which the mind recognizes as those that are present when you are normally enthusiastic and energetic, it will interpret them to mean that you *are* enthusiastic and energetic and respond accordingly—even if only moments ago you were sending signals which said you were tired.

No Time for Being Tired

You might say that this is only pretending to be energetic when you are really tired. But my question is this: Which state is real and which one isn't? Up until I learned to use this stuff, I had been quite an expert in the fine art of feeling rotten. I accomplished this unfortunate skill by habitually loading programs of tiredness and feeling rotten into my mind. Therefore, I was generally in a tired and rotten-feeling state, and it was certainly real to me. Then something happened that changed my understanding of things.

While going to college full-time, I was working as a caretaker in a residential care facility. Along with my regular eight-hour workdays, I worked alternate weekends consisting of two fifteen-hour shifts. It was quite a load, so my co-worker and I took it easy on the Fridays before these monster shifts. Once, on the Friday that ended finals week, I had experienced a grueling day at school and was absolutely wiped-out by the time it was over. Since I was so exhausted from studying and taking tests all week, the only thought on my mind as I was driving to work that afternoon was to get my co-worker to cover for me while I took a long nap. Our shift began fifteen minutes before our clients got home from their day program, and I usually got there about fifteen minutes before my co-worker did, so I was crashing on the sofa when the doorbell rang. I answered the door, and there was my supervisor, informing me that she was filling in for my co-worker. This was not good news.

My supervisor was of the drill sergeant variety, and she expected everything to be done properly, with enthusiasm, and no cutting any corners. On top of that, we didn't get along all that well, so she wasn't going to have any sympathy for my rough day. Instead of taking a nap and kicking back, I was going to have to do every learning and physical therapy program with the clients and no sitting down on the job. So, not having any say in the matter, that's what I did.

Well, a funny thing happened. After a few hours of non-stop running around and working with the clients, I noticed something: *I wasn't tired at all.* In fact, I was filled with energy for the remainder of the shift.

I'm not going to lie. If you had told me on my way to work that day that something like this was possible, I would have told you that you were insane. I wouldn't have believed you at all. And I would have been dead wrong.

Which State Was the "Real" State?

At the time, I didn't know anything about this rapid state-shifting from exhausted to energized. After my rough day, I did the normal thing and loaded my "feeling rotten" program into my mind's computer. But when my supervisor showed up, I was forced to load my "energy and enthusiasm" program instead. So there I was, filled with energy because that was the posture I had adopted (even though it was the *last* one I wanted to adopt at the time), and my mind reacted to the signals it was being sent.

Which state was the "real" one, the exhaustion I felt when I arrived, or the energetic one I was forced to adopt because of the circumstances? After all, I really did feel tired at the beginning of the shift, and I really did feel energized the whole time I was running around and working. By now I am hoping you know the answer: It doesn't matter. Your mind acts on the data it receives, regardless of whether it is "real" or not. Your reality is shaped by your beliefs. If you believe that you are tired, you will feel tired. If you get caught up in the moment and "forget" to feel tired, you won't be tired.

Twenty Dollars Says You're Not *Really* Tired
It really is that simple, but people have trouble believing that this is the case and are more than willing to fight it. One day, in the middle of a class discussion about this concept, I wasn't getting anywhere. It was just a big wall of resistance and I was really frustrated because of it. So I asked the kids who were tired to raise their hands and more than half the class did so. I asked these students if they were really tired, or just a little tired, and they all said they were *really* tired. They must have been, too, because all of them were displaying various postures of tiredness, slumped over and sitting there like lumps.

Pulling a twenty-dollar bill out of my wallet, I told them that it was unfortunate that they were so tired. I said that because I was so thirsty, I was willing to offer the change to whoever could get me a soda from the cafeteria and be back within two minutes. Without exception, each of the "really tired" students jumped up and insisted that they could do it, and that I should pick them. Putting the money back in my wallet, I told them that I just wanted to see how tired they really were. Seeing that they were ready willing and able to run across the school and back, I said it looked like they weren't tired at all, but filled with energy.

When they realized that I wasn't going to give the money away, they grumbled and went right back to the "tired" posture that they had started with. You can be sure they were just as "tired" then as they were "energized" a few seconds before when they thought they were going to get the money. In both cases they were absolutely correct.

Mental unwillingness to work
is accompanied by listlessness and lack of energy.
Enthusiasm and willingness
go hand in hand with fresh supplies of energy.
—*Paramahansa Yogananda*

Practice Your Posture of Success

Now that you have a better understanding of the effect that posture has on your state, use it to your advantage in your daily life. I've already discussed how to get into a state of energy and enthusiasm—you use your body as if you were already in that state. Do this enough and you will develop a habit of being in this state, and then you won't have to worry about the *as if* anymore because it will turn into an *I am.* If you are operating out of a state of energy and enthusiasm, the chances of your being successful improve dramatically.

So practice working with your posture. It's easy, and you can do it at any time. The next time you are walking to class, think of how you would be walking if you had just aced the hardest test you had ever taken, or had just been named most valuable player in your school's division, or had just won an award for best whatever it is you would want to win, and move that way. As soon as you do, you will feel a surge of confidence and energy. Please realize that it *isn't* fake. You feel it because you are sending signals of confidence and energy to your mind, and your mind is responding by sending back the same feelings.

Take advantage of the loop that is created between body and mind: The more you use your body to create a positive state, the more positive your state will be, and the more positive your state, the more you will use your body to maintain that state.

I cannot overemphasize the importance of learning to make this shifting of posture a habit. Being tired or not feeling well are two of the most prevalent excuses people use when they aren't doing as well as they know they could be doing. And these excuses are so easy to overcome. Please give this concept a fair shot because you can get so much benefit from it. With just a little investigation, you can lay an excellent and energetic foundation for accomplishing everything else you are going after.

Too Good to Be True?

I've said before that the things I am talking about in this book are simple, often deceptively so. I also pointed out the difference between simple and easy. (Walking a tightrope is simple, but not easy.) All of that still stands, but in this case I really do mean easy. The other stuff may be simple, but this element is simple *and* easy. You don't even have to practice. You can be good at it immediately and use it anytime you want. Just like that.

The only difficulty involved is in breaking down the wall that says it isn't possible and sincerely checking it out. Like Houdini in the unlocked cell or the elephant unable to break the rope, a lot of folks just cannot believe it is possible to make such dramatic changes in their energy level by just acting as if they had that energy. They won't even attempt it. And the saddest part is, this element is without doubt the easiest one to get the hang of *and* the easiest one to prove or disprove. So why not check it out? It only takes a minute or two, and the only thing you have to lose is a bunch of excuses.

> *Some men have thousands of reasons*
> *why they cannot do what they want to,*
> *when all they need is one reason why they can.*
> —*Willis Whitney*

We Use Self-Talk to Construct Our Reality

While posture plays a major part in state, it is only part of the story. Obviously, our mind plays a critical part in determining how we feel, and it does so in two primary ways. Much of our state comes from what we *say to ourselves* and how we represent, or *picture things*, in our mind.

When I was a classroom teacher, if there was one thing I did more than anything else every day, it would be telling people to stop talking. Every now and then, they actually did stop, at least out loud. But inside their heads it was different, wasn't it? You know what I'm talking about—that ever-present dialogue we are having with ourselves all day long. It never shuts up, does it? One of the names for this internal dialogue is self-talk, and it plays a central role in determining our state.

While much of the time we are merely babbling to ourselves about things that don't have much bearing on our lives either way, a good portion of what we say *does* make a difference. Different people talk about different things, and one of the things that separates those who consistently get successful results from those who keep getting rotten results, is the quality and overall direction of their internal conversations.

Self-talk is important because we do listen to it and use it to make sense of the world. Often, our conclusions about the way things are come from decisions we make during these conversations with ourselves. As we have seen from the example of John in the elevator, these conclusions are not based on what's actually happening on the outside, but on our representations or interpretations of what's going on.

In other words, we don't deal with reality itself, but with our version of reality, and an awful lot of our version of reality comes from what we literally *talk ourselves into.* This is why it's so easy to have two people with wildly different interpretations of the same event, as any detective talking to several witnesses of a crime will certainly tell you.

As with anything else, we fall into habitual patterns with our self-talk and don't always think about or pay conscious attention to what we are saying to ourselves. In fact, the majority of the time, we aren't even aware that we are doing it. Using our analogy of the mind being like a computer, think of these patterns as being computer programs. (Yes, this is similar to what I

said about beliefs being like software. Self-talk is a vital component in the development and reinforcement of beliefs, and works
the same way in the mind.) When you load a program into a
computer, the computer performs the functions without question. Likewise, your mind follows the directions it is given. It
doesn't stop and say, "Hey, this isn't right. This isn't true!" It
just acts on the information coming from the conversations you
are constantly having with yourself.

Self-Talk is Generally Negative
These habitual self-talk patterns can be hazardous if they are
made up of negative messages, and the sad part is that we often
get stuck in conversations with ourselves that are grounded in
pessimistic themes. "I'm really not that smart." "I'm not good
enough." "I'm tired." "I don't feel well." "I'm just not any good
at English." (Or history, or science, or writing, or spelling, or
math, or studying, or whatever.) "I suck at tests." "I always do
everything wrong." "I can't work under pressure." "I'm such an
idiot." "Things just don't work out for me." "This stuff isn't
going to work, either." "I'll never get ahead." "I'm lazy." "I'm
never going to get good grades." "This is so boring." "This is so
stupid." And let's not forget the worst one of all, the one that
gives us permission to hang on to all the other garbage: "That's
just the way I am!"

On and on this stuff goes and our minds just take it in
and produce the matching responses in our behavior. Whether
these thoughts are true or not makes absolutely no difference
whatsoever. Just like the elephant tied to the rope, if you believe
that's the way it is, then *that's the way it is.*

Negative Self-Talk Undermines Your Efforts to Improve

So what are the consistent messages that *you* are hearing? What programs are you playing day after day, week after week, year after year? The programs that you continually play determine the direction you move in because they set the mood you work from on a consistent basis. If the programs you load into your mind through your self-talk are negative, you can see what harm they are doing to you in your inability to achieve the results that you really want. After all, how can you be expected to get any positive work done over an extended period if you are constantly bombarding yourself with this kind of junk?

If you want to move in a positive direction, you'll want to start consciously playing some positive programs. It's not a matter of just thinking positively now and then; this stuff is programmed deeper than conscious thought. It's in your subconscious and you react to it automatically.

You know how it is. After every report card, you make a firm decision to do better *this* quarter, to do your homework, to study, to do everything on time, to stop messing around in class, etc. And it works for a couple of hours, days, or even a week or two. But then you fall into your same old patterns and start your same old habits all over again. Why?

Self-talk. Underneath your efforts to improve, you are still running negative programs through your internal dialogue, and the negative programs are going to win every time because they are more deeply ingrained. This is true for you, this is true for me, and this is true for everyone who has had these scripts programmed in. The "why" has as many variations as there are people. The "what" is the same story for everyone.

Self-Talk Won't Just Shut Up

To turn things around, you can't just stop the programs. Your mind thrives on self-talk, and if you want to experience sheer frustration, just try to get your self-talk to shut up. It's not going to. Stopping your self-talk isn't the answer because some program *will* be played.

The key to changing your negative self-talk programs is just that—change them. What you want to do is to replace the old, negative program with a more consciously directed positive program. Again, it's just like beliefs: If you are running a program that says, "I'm lazy and can't get my work done," you need to consciously and consistently replace it with the opposite program that you would rather have, which is some version of, "I'm a hard worker and I get the job done." If you are running a program that insists you that you can't do well on tests, turn it around and begin running one that tells your mind that you *can* do well on tests because you are prepared and confident.

You are What You are,
But Who Says You Have to Stay that Way?

If I suggest changing your self-talk programs, there's a part of you that may say, "Hey, I can't do that; it's a lie. I really *am* lazy." (Or whatever.) Well, sure you are, *if* that's the program you consistently run. But were you born lazy? Were you born stupid? Were you born a procrastinator? Don't bother answering because these questions are as ridiculous as they sound.

So what can you do to move beyond these programs? Let's face it: If you are dealing with any of these issues, all that you've done is talk yourself *into* your present state over a period of time and found reasons to reinforce your beliefs. You may have had lots of help from others, but so it goes. I did, too. It isn't right, it isn't fair, and it *isn't* final. Regardless of why you've talked yourself into your state or how long you've been doing so, you can talk yourself *out* of it, too. You just have to be willing to work at it.

There's no rule that says you have to stay the way you believe yourself to be right now. If you want to change, you can. The reality of a situation is what you make it. If you change your state, *reality* has a way of changing right along with you. Remember, you react to what you *think* is going on, not reality itself. But it sure does seem real to you, doesn't it?

> *Be careful how you interpret the world: It is like that.*
> *—Erich Heller*

Taking Control of Something You Already Do Daily

Also, if the idea of working with your self-talk programs seems strange, or if you're not sure that you can do it, don't worry. As with all of the techniques in this book, you are already doing it. You are not learning how to do anything new here. You are just taking conscious control of something you've been doing all of your life. It's not the skill that's new here, but the idea that you are doing it deliberately instead of having it just happen to you without your being aware of it.

Of course, if you don't do it intentionally, you will still be doing it anyway; you just won't be doing it consciously, and you will not have control of your state. It's kind of like being on a boat out at sea. If the wind is blowing and you have your sail up, you have control over the direction in which you travel. If you take down your sail, you don't affect the wind, you just lose control over the direction you will move.

The wind is going to blow whether your sail is up or not. Self-talk is like the wind. It's going on whether you are paying attention to it or not. The only question is whether you are going to control the direction in which it is going to move you.

> *Take charge of your thoughts.*
> *You can do what you will with them.*
> *—Plato*

Guidelines for Changing Old Self-Talk Programs

Ok, so how do you change your programs? We've already mentioned the key ingredients, so let's set them out in order. (If you think this sounds a lot like the belief guidelines, good. Nice to see that you are paying attention.)

One: Find the negative programs you want to replace

If you can spot your negative programs easily, fine. Sometimes, however, it's not that easy to get a handle on them because they generally work in the unconscious mind. But don't worry if you can't come up with them right away. They will either show up as you begin your work, or your new programs will overwrite them if you program the new ones effectively.

The important thing for you to do is to determine the areas that you want to concentrate on in order for you to successfully achieve the goals you are pursuing. This is about taking control of stuff that is happening anyway, whether you are paying attention to it or not. So look at your goals and see if you can spot any self-talk patterns that are holding you back.

A good way to spot a negative program is to simply take your goal and ask yourself, "Why can't I accomplish this?" After you have asked the question, listen to your mind's response. If there are negative programs connected with this area, they will probably make themselves known as objections, fears, or reservations. Don't shut them out, though. Give them the voice they want. You may not want them there, but that's not the same thing as them not being there, is it? Denying these programs is not the answer; changing them is.

Two: Find the positive programs to use as replacements

Look at the negative programs that you discovered when examining your goals and consider what the opposite programs would be. Be sure to frame them in language that is positive and that concentrates on what you want to accomplish, instead of what you want to avoid.

For example, if you are designing a program to overcome feelings of inadequacy when it comes to getting all of your assignments done, you would want a program that says something like, "I have what it takes to get my assignments done on time." Also, as I've said when discussing identity, beliefs, and visualization, don't worry if you don't feel that you've been behaving in this way up to this point.

Your previous self-talk has put limits on your behavior, and changes in your self-talk will reinforce your new belief. As you work, you will see a positive loop form: positive self-talk creates positive results create positive self-talk creates . . .

Together, these elements create a new belief that reinforces your new identity, which further strengthens the whole process. Yes, as I keep saying, this stuff all works together.

Three: Be consistent in your practice

Like everything else, the more you practice your positive self-talk, the better you are going to get at it. Remember what you are doing here.

You are working toward replacing negative programs that may have been running for years. This replacement isn't going to happen with just one or two attempts. You've got to keep at it. It *is* going to take some time, but fortunately, you will be working deliberately, and you will be doing this work in conjunction with other techniques.

This concentration of effort and techniques will make things happen in a much faster time frame than the haphazard way that you initially did these things when you weren't consciously paying attention to what you were doing.

Be as consistent and diligent in your practice as you can. It isn't hard, and it doesn't take a lot of time. It only takes regularity. The few minutes you spend each day will pay off a thousand times over and will continue to bring you rewards long after you are out of school because these elements can be applied to whatever area of your life you want to improve.

Four: Find a regular time to practice

First thing in the morning and before you go to bed are both excellent times to work at this, just like with visualization, but you can do it anytime that is comfortable for you. Just make sure that you are as consistent as possible because we are creatures of habit. (Ok, so we are mostly creatures of bad habits, but we're out to change that, aren't we?) The more consistent you are with practicing at regular times, the easier it is to establish the habit of practice. This habit is something you definitely want to install. You know how easy it is to get swept away in everyday events and forget to do something because of all the stuff that constantly grabs at your attention. Also, without a clearly established practice routine, it is easy to get caught up in the, "Oh, I'll do it tomorrow" rut. Tomorrow and tomorrow and tomorrow. Days, weeks, and months can slip by this way, and soon you can find yourself in the same place that you were last year: almost just about ready to finally begin to get started on commencing to get this stuff together.

So work the best you can to set up a regular routine. Then, if you want to do extra work with the techniques when you have a minute, all the better. Additional practice strengthens your gains, but without the regular routine, you will find it difficult to be consistent.

Homeostasis

There is another good reason why you should work to establish a regular routine. Unfortunately, it's the same reason why you might find it hard to do so in the first place. There's something called homeostasis, and it plays a major part in our lives. Homeostasis is any system's tendency to remain stable by resisting changes or disruptions, and it's one reason why it is hard to make lasting changes in your routine. A simple definition would be: This is the way it's been, so let's keep it this way.

Homeostasis is usually discussed in relation to biology because it is an important element in keeping the different bodily systems functioning properly. An example of homeostasis is the body's immune system fighting off a disease or the healing of a cut. But homeostasis applies to systems of all kinds, whether they are institutions, governments, or your usual routine.

We all have regular routines, and homeostasis works to keep those routines going. This is why, for example, it is hard at first for people to lose weight, or to keep it off once they do. When any change is introduced into the system, in this case the system being your routine behavior, there is a degree of resistance to it.

Your initial efforts to alter your behavior will be met with resistance, due to homeostasis. But if you keep at it, the same homeostasis will begin to help you maintain your new routine. For this to happen, however, you will have to be consistent. If you only do it sporadically, your chances of maintaining the changes you want will not be good because of homeostasis.

Therefore, if homeostasis can be either your enemy or your ally, why not choose to make it your ally? Instead of continuing to play the negative programs and wondering why you aren't getting anywhere, be consistent with the programming of your positive self-talk. You will find yourself working from a positive, resourceful state with greater frequency than you might have thought possible.

Motivation is what gets you started.
Habit is what keeps you going.
—Jim Ryun

If You Don't Like Reality, Reframe It

Remember, we don't really experience the reality of any given situation; we interpret the situation based on the filters consisting of our beliefs, focus, and state. Our state is determined by what we associate to the things that happen to us, not by the things themselves. These associations are the frame through which we see the picture of the event.

If we change the frame, we can change the way we feel about things. This is what happened to John in the elevator. Initially, he was angry because he thought someone was being rude to him. But when he saw the old woman, he changed his associations from ones of anger at someone being mean to ones of compassion for an old woman. This process of changing associations is called reframing because the frame is the meaning that we associate to the event. If we shift the frame, we shift the meaning, and ultimately, our state.

I've learned from experience
that the greater part of our happiness or misery
depends on our dispositions and not on our circumstances.
—Martha Washington

Most folks are about as happy as they make up their minds to be.
—Abraham Lincoln

Do Some Situations Have a Definite Meaning? Maybe

Some might say that certain situations have obvious meaning, that there are definite responses that one should have in reaction to them. They would say that in the elevator story, John obviously and certainly would have helped the old woman. Perhaps, but there is an old story from China that deals with the "obvious" and "certain" meaning of events.

There was an old farmer who lived in a poor village. He was better off than most of the villagers, since he had a horse to help him work his land. One day, his horse ran away and the other villagers lamented about how unfortunate this was. The farmer only replied, "maybe."

After a few days, the horse came back to the farm, and along with it were two wild horses. This time, the villagers were pleased about the farmer's good fortune, but all he said was, "maybe."

Excited about the new horses, the farmer's son tried to ride one. He was thrown from the beast, breaking his leg. The villagers were quick to offer their condolences, since this meant that the son could not help his father work the farm. The farmer only replied, "maybe."

A few days later, officers from the military came to the village looking for young men to draft into the army. Because the farmer's son had a broken leg, he wasn't drafted. When the villagers told the farmer how lucky he was, he only replied, "maybe."

Reframing Allows You to Tap Greater Resources

Not many of us have the ability to look at events so evenly. In a similar situation, most of us would regard a broken leg or a lost horse as bad news, and two new horses or not being drafted as good news. But this doesn't mean that these events automatically come with these "obvious" meanings, as the farmer was wise enough to see. Usually, when something happens we rush to assign a meaning to the event and then base our reactions on that meaning. But we *are* only reacting to our interpretation.

There's an often told story about a guy from IBM who made a mistake on a business deal that resulted in the company losing several million dollars. He was called into the office of Tom Watson, the company founder, and before Watson could say anything, the guy says, "I know that you're going to fire me, but . . ." Watson's eyes widened and he said, "*Fire* you? Are you crazy? I've just spent millions training you!"

Now, *that's* reframing.

> *Men are disturbed not by things,*
> *but by the view which they take of them.*
> —*Epictetus*

Learning to Reframe Mistakes

This idea of reframing is critical when you've made a mistake. Normally, when we look back on mistakes, we get upset or feel embarrassed. But in general, don't we learn more from our mistakes than we do from the good stuff that we do? After all, when things are going along smoothly, we tend to cruise right along with them. When we screw up, we pay more attention because we have to think about what we did wrong in order to make sure that we don't have to go through the same thing again. Since the meaning of an incident is entirely up to you, you can either emphasize the fact that you made a mistake, or you can reframe it and emphasize the value that comes from your learning something useful.

This does *not* mean pretending that everything is wonderful, because sometimes things aren't wonderful at all, are they? But some of the most significant victories you will ever have will come in the face of difficulty. It's not in saying that everything is wonderful that reframing has its value, but in the ability to look at a situation and see what can be gained from it to help you succeed in achieving your goals. Can you see how this is directly connected to having a positive focus? Again, it doesn't mean thinking everything is great; it means getting the best out of a situation, even if the situation isn't any good at all.

> *Things turn out best for people*
> *who make the best of the way things turn out.*
> —*John Wooden*

A great little trick that is related to mistakes and your state is learning to shift out of "idiot-mode" and back into a state that is more productive. When you screw something up and start feeling like an idiot, stop for a few seconds and go and do something else that you know you can do well. It doesn't have to be a big thing, or anything involved or complicated. You only need a few seconds. Just make it something you are good at. In fact, you don't even need to actually do it; you can just visualize it for a few seconds. This is an effective way of regrouping, of shifting your state away from an, "Oh, I'm such an idiot" mode and putting it back in a, "See, I can do this" state. Then you can return to what you were doing with a better state of mind and get better results. Remember the emotional radio dial: *If you don't like the music, change the station.*

Ask and You Shall Receive

There is another effective way to change your state that most people won't even investigate because they think it couldn't possibly be that simple. But it is, *if* you practice. As I keep saying over and over, these elements are simple, taken by themselves. But when you start putting them to work with each other, the results can be amazing. It just takes practice and the ability to go for it again if you screw up at first. It all happens in little steps, the smallest of which brings big results when followed by another small step. Don't worry if you mess up, or forget to do something, or fall back into an old pattern. Just get back to business and keep going.

> *Fall seven times, stand up eight.*
> —*Japanese Proverb*

So if you want to change your state, there is a simple way to do it: just ask. That's right, just ask and your mind will show you how. When you get in a situation that you don't care for, like an English class, or math class, or whatever, instead of falling into the old automatic responses, just pose a more powerful question: "How can I have a better focus here?" Or, "how can I improve my state?" If you really want to do it, and aren't just asking half-heartedly, your mind will show you an angle you hadn't considered before. Look, lots of people, even though they are miserable most of the time, are happy to stay as they are. After all, there is a tremendous benefit to being able to blame everything on somebody or something else: They don't have to take responsibility for themselves. Classic secondary gain.

But if you truly want to change your focus, your mind will be happy to help you, if you only ask it how. If you think this sounds funny, stop for a second. Do you realize how often your mind has supplied you with reasons why you should have been in a rotten state? Do you realize how often you've been ready and willing to go right along with the reasons you received? "Why does this always happen to me?" "Why are people such idiots?" "Why do I have to do this stupid stuff?" "How am I going to survive until the end of this class?" Should it be so hard to get reasons why you should have a positive state? It isn't. Get into the habit of asking questions that lead your mind to come up with these reasons, and do it on a daily basis. The more you do it, the easier it becomes and the stronger your habit of accessing positive states becomes.

Your mind is going to give you an answer to the questions you ask it, whether these questions are positive or negative. If you get in the habit of asking yourself questions like, "How can I be more enthusiastic?," as opposed to, "Why do I have to do this stupid stuff?," you will experience states that are far superior to the ones that come with the negative questions. It really is a matter of ask and you shall receive.

If You Don't Appreciate What You Have Now,
Why Will You Appreciate What You Have Later?

It's so easy to be dissatisfied with what we have or who we are, given all the avenues of disenchantment that are there for us to walk along. I mentioned before that the media does a lot to train us to have a negative focus. One of the main roles of advertising in general is to leave you feeling incomplete unless you have the particular item that the commercial or ad is telling you to buy, regardless of whether you need it or not. We want the things others have, so we are dissatisfied. We want to be what others are, so we are dissatisfied. All too often, it seems like if it isn't *something else*, we don't want it.

If we don't want to get bogged down in this negativity, we've got to be able to appreciate the things that we have within our grasp, even as we are reaching for something else. Appreciation, although it often goes unappreciated, is an essential ingredient in the recipe for a positive state. Too often, however, it is confused with just accepting things the way they are.

A certain amount of discontent isn't a bad thing because it spurs us on to achieve more. But it's important to strike a balance. Just because I am not content with my situation and want to improve upon it, doesn't mean that I don't appreciate what the situation provides me. It's like a bridge across a raging river in a storm. I may not be content to remain on the bridge, but I certainly do appreciate the fact that it is there to allow me to cross the river.

We take so much for granted on a daily basis, but we don't have to be this way. Of course, the point isn't for us to feel guilty about what we have or for wanting to do better than we are. After all, this book is dedicated to helping you improve your resources, your skills, and your situation. It's not wrong to want things to be better than they are, but it *is* wrong not to appreciate what you have while you strive to accomplish your goals. The reason why it is wrong is that if you are not grateful for what you have now there's little chance that you will appreciate what you have later.

Nothing is enough to the man for whom enough is too little.
—Epicurus

People often believe that if they could only get ____, *then* they would be happy. This is one of the biggest fallacies that we can fall into, and it always comes down to state. If we fail to appreciate what we've got now, we stand little chance of feeling better about what comes along later because our focus will already be trained on the negative.

Since every new situation will always and inevitably have negative aspects to it, (every front has a back, every in has an out, every up has a down, etc.) our negative focus will lock onto them, and we will be in the miserable state of, "Ok, this is almost pretty good, but what I *really* want is . . ." Is that where you perpetually want to be? If not, don't lose sight of the things that you have to be grateful for, even as you strive to gain more.

The Stonecutter

Despite the many ways that times have changed, this failure to appreciate what we have or where we are isn't a new condition. In fact, there's another old Chinese story that sums it up perfectly, the story of the stonecutter.

Once, there was a stonecutter who was unhappy with his lot in life. He hated the fact that he was only a poor stonecutter and he resented just about everyone. He was out walking one day, and upon passing a rich merchant's house, he looked in and saw the exquisite furnishings and influential visitors. He became bitter. "If only *I* were a wealthy merchant," he thought, "I could live like *this* and wouldn't have to be a lowly stonecutter."

To his astonishment, his wish was instantly granted and he became a merchant, wealthier and more powerful than the one he had begrudged. Now, *he* was envied and hated by those who were less powerful, and this made him glad.

But then he heard a commotion and saw a government official being carried through the streets on a sedan chair escorted by soldiers. Regardless of how wealthy they were, everyone had to bow down as the official's entourage passed. "What if *I* were a government official? Then, everyone would have to bow down to *me!*"

Suddenly, he became a powerful government official with an even larger entourage. Now, *he* was being carried around the streets in a lavishly decorated sedan chair while the people bowed low in envy and fear. But it was a hot day, and in his official regalia, he began sweating profusely. In his discomfort, he glanced at the sun and cursed his tormentor, which just shone steadily, unaffected by the official or his procession. "If *I* could be the sun," he said, "then I would be powerful, indeed!"

Lo and behold, without warning, he became the sun. Now, *he* was shining down furiously upon the town and wilting the crops in the fields. Townspeople and countryfolk, lord and peasant alike—all swore at him with raised fists, but to no avail. All of a sudden, however, a great dark cloud came between him and the earth, and he could no longer menace the people below. "This storm cloud is more powerful than I. If *I* were a storm cloud, I could rain down upon all!"

Now *he* was a storm cloud, letting loose his fury. Great torrents of rain flooded the land, and the people cursed him mightily. But then he found that he was being moved along by a great gust of wind. "I cannot believe the power of this wind," he thought. "If *I* were the wind, there would be no limit to my might!"

And so it happened. *He* was the wind, and oh, how he blew across the land. Trees were cast down, houses were blown over—none could stand his fury, and all were afraid and hated him. However, there was one thing that could resist his onslaught. Alone in a field stood a gigantic boulder, towering over the countryside. It would not be harmed, no matter how hard he blew. "Oh, if *I* could be this mighty rock, nothing could avail against *me!*"

So *he* was the boulder, lord of the countryside. There he sat, proud and powerful, until a day came when he heard one clink and then another, like a hammer and chisel, and he realized he was losing something of his power. He shouted, "What is going on here?" But the hammering continued, regardless of his protest. There at his base was a humble stonecutter, whistling contentedly as he chiseled.

The hardest arithmetic to master
is that which enables us to count our blessings.
—*Eric Hoffer*

Anchors a Long Way Up the Dial

Ever had this happen? There you are, going along feeling fine, and then without anything happening that you can put your fingering on, *boom*—you're in a funk and feeling down. If so, it's possible that you had an anchor triggered without knowing it. Anchors are learned responses where something in our experience automatically triggers an emotional response, whether we are conscious of the connection or not. Something happens on the outside to make you feel something on the inside, only you aren't always aware of what has happened or why.

A classic example of an anchor is when you have a song that you associate with a certain person. When you hear that song, you not only are reminded of that person, but you also experience strong emotions connected to that person. Whether the emotions are positive or negative depends on the relationship you have with the person.

Although anchors generally happen unconsciously, it is possible to develop conscious anchors as well, and that's what I'm going to show you how to do here. This is a simple technique you can use to adjust your state in situations where you need a quick move "up the dial" from wherever you are at the moment. By aligning a simple physical gesture to the feelings felt during a positive experience, you can take advantage of the mind/body connection and experience a similar state. Believe me, this can come in awfully handy (like before you have to take a test or something.) Having "tuned your dial" to a more positive "station," you can then continue on in the same situation, experiencing it from the higher spot on the dial.

Here's how you do it: First, choose a simple gesture to use as the anchor. The gesture itself is not that important. It just has to be something you don't normally do. For example, I am not in the habit of tugging on my earlobe, so I could use that, but I do have a habit of drumming my fingers on my knee when I am sitting down, so I don't want to use that. Whatever it is that you use, make it something simple and out of the ordinary.

Next, choose a positive experience you have had in the past. It doesn't matter if it was a big deal or important; the only thing that matters is that it resulted in a highly positive state, that it made you feel really, *really* good when you experienced it. For example, I could create an anchor using my hike up that mountain trail that I talked about back in the Goals chapter.

Once you've chosen the experience you are going to use, replay the "video" of that experience in your mind to the best of your ability. Go back and relive the experience as clearly as you can, seeing as many details as you can and making it as vivid as possible—just as if you were watching a video of the experience. But instead of just "watching" it, as if from a distance, relive it as if it were happening *right now*, experiencing the feelings you felt at the time. When you get to the part you enjoyed the most, the peak of the experience, make the gesture you chose.

Just watch the "video" and when you get to the peak, make the gesture. That's all there is to it, and as you can see, it isn't difficult to do. But like other elements here, the key is in the repetition. The more you do it (with attention and deep feeling, of course) the stronger the anchor becomes.

Go through the process a few times each day and soon you will have anchored it into your consciousness. Then, after it is anchored in, whenever you want to experience the state that you have anchored, you can make the gesture and your mind will move toward that state. This is a pretty good deal, isn't it? You do *this*, you get *that*. Check it out.

State is the key to how you feel and state is determined by your reaction to, or associations regarding, the events and circumstances *out there* in that "real" world we hear so much about.

Since you determine your state, it's in your best interest to manage it by learning how to habitually access resourceful, empowering states instead of negative, disempowering ones. The choice is yours and you now have a number of tools to work with. The only thing we need to deal with now is that killer of too many dreams—fear.

Enthusiasm is the mother of effort,
and without it nothing great was ever achieved.
Ralph Waldo Emerson

Enthusiasm is the greatest asset in the world.
It beats money, power, and influence.
—Henry Chester

Nothing can stop the man with the right mental attitude
from achieving his goal;
nothing on earth can help the man
with the wrong mental attitude.
—Thomas Jefferson

Chapter Seven

Fear, Failure, and Other Fun Stuff—
I'm Afraid We May Experience Some Delays

Most of our obstacles would melt away
if, instead of cowering before them,
we should make up our minds to walk boldly through them.
—Orison Swett Marden

Ok, so it's time to get moving. You agree that this all makes sense, you understand how it works, you've figured out what you want to do, you're excited about the possibilities, you know what to do, and . . . nothing happens. Day after day goes by and you've found one more reason why *tomorrow* would be the best day to get started. Things come up, extremely important things, sure, but when you finally get finished with them, you're going to get to work. Tomorrow.

What's going on here? If you find yourself stuck in any variation of the above dilemma, you may start to think that you are going crazy, but don't worry. You're not alone. Many of us, when embarking on any kind of new project, are bound to run up against that great brake on the wheels of any kind of progress we might desire—fear. Remember homeostasis, a system's built in resistence to change? Fear is its best friend.

Fear defeats more people
than any other one thing in the world.
—Ralph Waldo Emerson

Fear is Useful, But at What Price?

Although sometimes it seems like everyone else is just cruising along untouched while *you* are the only one affected by it, the truth is that everyone experiences fear because it's part of our wiring. It has a vital part to play. Fear is a survival tool, and a really good one. Like any tool, however, it can be misused. After all, a hammer, useful as it is, is probably not the best thing for buttering your bread. So, even though we often hear the idea that we should have no fear, don't forget that it is necessary and built into the system.

In its intended function, fear helps us survive, but it does so at a price. Our sense of fear alerts us to trouble and prompts us to adopt one of two primary modes: *fight* or *flight.* When we encounter a threatening situation, we either stay and punch it out or we run away. It is fear that triggers the tremendous flow of adrenaline that allows us to perform at levels that we do not usually work from.

You've probably heard of incidents like some mother lifting up a car because her child was trapped underneath and other examples. It's rarely that extreme, of course, but fear accelerates the system's functions. While it is surely helpful when we have our backs against the wall, it takes a toll on the body. Our heart rate and breathing quicken, our blood pressure rises, and our stress level goes way up. Too much of it too often and it can harm to the system.

We Get Too Many Frights From Maybes and Mights

Since there is so much strain placed on the system by fear, it's preferable not to indulge in it unless it's necessary, meaning a *real* threat. But the truth is that we spend a lot of time fearing things that aren't even there.

How much of what we fear is real? We fear things that *may* take place—*if* this or that happens. We spend so much time worrying about things that *might* happen, fearing the *possible* circumstances and the *probable* results. Much of what we spend so much energy worrying about might not even come to pass. "What if I don't pass this test?" "What if I don't get the grades I want?" "What if I don't make the team?" "What if no one asks me to go to the prom?" "What if she won't go to the prom with me?" "What will my parents say when I get home?" "What if my friends find out about . . . ?" I'm sure that if you stopped and thought about it, you could come up with many examples of situations where you spent a good deal of time worrying about something that you were afraid was going to happen and it never did. Here's a little acronym to help you remember this point: False Evidence Appearing Real.

> *We are more often frightened than hurt;*
> *and we suffer more from imagination than from reality.*
> *—Seneca*

These "maybe it will happen" fears wouldn't be that big of a deal if the body could tell what's real or not. But the fact is that it cannot. If fear is triggered, your body reacts *as if* the thing you were afraid of *was* real. It goes through the same strain that it would go through if the situation actually did happen. This strain drains your body of energy. It makes you tired and unable to put out the necessary effort to succeed. You become anxiety-ridden and stressed out to the point where you cannot function at your best. In fact, you can't even function at your second or third best. Fear saps you. It weakens you and robs you of your purpose.

> *You gain strength, courage, and confidence by every experience*
> *in which you really stop to look fear in the face.*
> —*Eleanor Roosevelt*

Fear Doesn't Help You Solve Anything

These disadvantages might be worth putting up with, *if* this state of fear produced results that were helpful in overcoming the situation or condition that was feared. But on top of the abuse fear renders on body and mind, it does nothing to help alleviate the problem. All it does is put the brakes on the resources you do have that would help you solve the problem. To further compound the problem, repetition of this action of fearing what "might happen" soon develops into a habit of fear. Then, whenever a situation comes up where the outcome is uncertain (which is only about twelve times a day, right?) your chances of accessing this state of fear are very good, and without even thinking about it, you find yourself anxious and working from a deficit. Great deal, isn't it?

In its proper capacity, fear serves as an alarm system to help you recognize danger. But just like any alarm system, once you are alerted to the danger, you turn the thing off and do something to deal with the situation. The alarm system itself doesn't do anything to work out a solution, does it?

When we develop the habit of fear, we are operating with the alarm on much of the time. Imagine how difficult it would be to come up with favorable solutions with a car alarm blaring in your ear. It's not that much different with the alarm of fear constantly sounding when you are trying to get things done in your everyday life. Of course, after you get used to it, it doesn't seem so loud, but it still stops you from thinking straight.

Fear is static that prevents me from hearing myself.
—Samuel Butler

Fear Controls Your Focus

As if this weren't enough, fear also has another delightful characteristic: It goes a long way toward helping you bring about the very condition or situation you fear. It does this by controlling your focus. Let's say there is a big test that you are going to have next week. You have options as to how you could approach it. A good one would be to figure out what was necessary in order to prepare for it properly. You could find out what was on it and systematically attack the material with a positive attitude, excited about the challenge of doing well because that's what you do, you do well on tests.

On the other hand, you could take the more common, fear-based approach. The first thing you do is stress out and start worrying about how you're going to bomb this test your stupid teacher is going to torture you with. You don't study that much because you don't have a prayer anyway, so what's the use?

As the test date nears, your sense of panic demands that you try to study some, so you hit the books and immediately get confused because you're not sure what to do. After all, you don't have a lot of time and you have other things to do, too. When the day arrives, you're unprepared, you're tired, and you don't feel well. You spend most of your time staring at stuff you have no idea how to do, and of course, you bomb the thing. Which is just what you were afraid of in the first place, wasn't it?

It all comes back to focus. When you get into a fearful state, what do you do? You put your focus on the problem instead of on the solution. Fear controls your focus. If you are afraid of something, you will spend a lot of time and energy concentrating on it. Instead of doing something positive to prepare for doing well, your fear forces you to focus on what can go wrong. Since you are looking at the negative possibilities with such intensity, your self-talk will certainly begin running your, "I'm going to fail, I *know* I'm going to fail" program. This brings in stress, which burns you out and takes away from your ability to work effectively. So you wind up getting exactly the kind of results you were afraid of getting in the first place. Which gives you a chance to cling tightly to your identity as someone who fails at this type of thing because *that's the way you are,* which reinforces your negative visualization, which stops you from setting any goals that would help you stem the tide, which helps you focus on what can go wrong, which starts the whole negative loop all over again. What a ride.

The thing we fear we bring to pass.
—Elbert Hubbard

Replacing the Habit of Fear With the Habit of Success

It should be clear by now that chronic fear is not your friend. So what can you do about it? Hopefully, you now have a better understanding of what chronic fear is and how it works against you. While that's not enough to solve the problem, it *is* a sound beginning. Fear becomes a little less powerful when it is exposed to the light of understanding. As far as the habit of fear goes, you've got to realize that it's just like any other habit. If you want to change it, you've got to reprogram it. Fortunately, this book contains tools that will help you succeed in doing just that. If you consistently work with the information provided here, you will begin to see such results that much of what you were afraid of will simply lose its hold on you because your newly formed habits will prove to you that you can indeed accomplish many of the things you were afraid of attempting in the past.

But like I said at the beginning of the chapter, it is exactly this habit of fear that can so often get in the way of your seriously working with this stuff. One of the most pervasive fears—and one that is quite effective at stopping us from committing to anything—is the fear of failure.

The Road to Success is Lined With Failures

We're all familiar with the fears associated with failure. It's like we don't want to let ourselves down, or set ourselves up for disappointment. All too often, we become afraid of the possibility of failure, so much so that we won't even attempt something, even though we really want the results it would bring. What do we gain by this? Nothing. It's like the old saying: People who don't make mistakes don't make anything.

Behold the turtle:
He only makes progress when he sticks his neck out.
—James Bryant Conant

None of us likes failing, but the real question is: what will we do when we *do* fail? Most people give up after a failure or two, figuring that they don't have what it takes to succeed at that particular task or in that kind of situation. This isn't the best thinking because like it or not, failure is part of the game. As any person who is successful at anything will verify, there are numerous failures on the way to success.

As an example, look at baseball. Being inducted into the Hall of Fame is certainly a reliable measure of success, isn't it? If a player has a lifetime batting average of .300, it's a safe bet that he is going to wind up in the Hall of Fame. Well, guess what? A .300 hitter *fails* seven times out of ten. That's right, even the best hitters in the game fail more than twice as many times as they succeed.

Another area of greatness is in hitting home runs. If you look at the all-time home run leaders, there's an interesting parallel. Babe Ruth, Reggie Jackson, and Mike Schmidt, to name three, are also among the all-time leaders in strikeouts. Nobody seems to pay much attention to that, though. The point of this is that success doesn't come without failure. You've got to be willing to fail if you want to succeed, so please don't let the possibility of failure stop you from beginning something.

The only true failure lies in the failure to start.
—Harold Blake Walker

Past Failures Have Nothing to Do With the Future

Much of our fear of failure comes from past experience, which shouldn't come as much of a surprise, should it? After all, if you have done poorly at something before, it's easy to doubt that you will be able to do much better in the future. But the only power your past performance has on your ability to succeed now is what you choose to give it through limiting beliefs. If you align the elements of achievement and let go of the idea that you can't do it now because you couldn't do it before, you will greatly increase your chances of success.

History is filled with stories of those who failed often before they finally succeeded, and an illuminating one is that of Thomas Edison. Even though he is known for inventing the lightbulb, he really didn't. What he did do, however, was come up with the first practical, long-lasting bulb suitable for public use. Along the way, however, he had a bit of problem of finding the right material to use for the filament, that little wire inside. It's said that he tried over *ten thousand* times before he found one that would work properly. When someone asked him how he felt about failing, he said, "I am not discouraged, because every wrong attempt discarded is another step forward."

I am not concerned that you have fallen;
I am concerned that you arise.
—Abraham Lincoln

Success is the ability to go from one failure to another
with no loss of enthusiasm.
—Sir Winston Churchill

Let's Say You've Failed a Lot in the Past

Are *you* going to be deterred by past failures? Are you afraid to set goals because you don't think you can achieve them? Are you worried that you cannot achieve the goals you might want to set because you haven't done well in those areas before?

Look: Maybe you have done poorly in school up to this point and are having trouble seeing yourself doing well in the future. If so, here are some questions to consider:

+ What identity were you working with?
+ What kind of student did you see yourself as?
+ What belief structure were you working under?
+ What habits were you stuck in?
+ How clear was your idea about what you were going after?
+ What kind of focus did you have on a day-to-day basis?
+ What states were you routinely working from?
+ How fired up were you about doing well?

If you are honest with yourself, I think you will see that you haven't been giving yourself half the chance you could have been giving yourself. Maybe you didn't put out half the effort you could have, or were flat out working against yourself without even knowing it. In fact, the worse the answers to these questions, the better the news. After all, having come this far, you now know a world of information that you either didn't know before, or if you did know it, didn't know how to integrate usefully into your day to day routine.

If you've started to work on any of the areas that the above questions touch on, using the techniques provided here, don't you think your chances of succeeding are going to improve? As I've said from the start, it's not like I just made any of this stuff up. It *works*. So many people have gotten remarkable results in so many different areas of achievement by using this same information. *You* can get similar results in your studies and whatever else you choose to turn your attention toward.

If at this point, you still don't believe that you can get A's, if you are saying to yourself that all of this sounds good for somebody else, but *you* have been getting F's or D's or C's, and you're just not good enough, or smart enough, you must remember that getting the grades isn't nearly so much a matter of being smart enough as it is a matter of getting rid of the baggage that you've programmed into your mind.

Take out the garbage and replace it with the belief that you *can* do what needs to be done. The results you get will conform to whatever program you consistently run. Fortunately, you now know what to do to begin running positive, empowering programs. What you've done before has little bearing on what you can do today and tomorrow, *if* you are committed to improving.

Forget past mistakes. Forget failures.
Forget everything except what you are going to do now and do it.
—William Durant

What's So Comfortable About the Comfort Zone?
Another sort of fear associated with the inability to really get going with this stuff is the fear of breaking out of your comfort zone, something we are generally resistant to doing. As I said in

Chapter Four when discussing goals, our comfort zone is the area of behavior, either in thought or action, where we feel comfortable. Comfort zones are based on familiarity. If we are used to something, if a situation or condition holds little in the way of surprises, we tend to be at ease, or comfortable with it.

It's important to understand that comfort zones aren't necessarily made up of things that we would ordinarily associate with comfort. It is quite possible for someone to have a comfort zone consisting of negative elements. Certainly an extreme example, but one that should get the point across, is the case of someone who has spent time in prison, has just gotten out, and does something to go back because he can't deal with life on the outside.

While inside, he had a great amount of structure and control. He was told what to do and when to do it, and knew exactly what would happen if he didn't. This becomes routine, and although it cannot in any way be described as pleasant, it is comfortable, at least as far as familiarity goes. In other words, the experience becomes secure in that it can be relied upon.

As this person gets out, all of the structure, the routine, the control, and the security is removed. Now on his own in a world that does not provide the reliability of the prison environment, he soon finds that he cannot cope with the lack of dependable routine. So, as crazy as it sounds, he winds up doing something that lands him right back in prison, back within the confines of his comfort zone.

Of course, most of us do not have comfort zones that are as severe as the above example, but they *can* be very much like a prison. This is because they are built with the bars of limiting ideas, beliefs, and habits, many of which were developed a long time ago and have been unchallenged ever since. (Remember the elephant and the rope?) So when something comes along to challenge us or attempt to pull us out of our comfort zone, we resist it, fear it, hate it, flee it, or any combination of these. We don't like feeling uncomfortable, so we fight to stay where things are familiar. The weird thing is, we often do it even if this familiar place is not necessarily where we think we want to be. We do it even if what we are resisting will ultimately help us get the things we do want.

Can you see why you might be having trouble getting going with this stuff? Whatever is going on with you right now, it's familiar. Even if you are unhappy with the results you're getting in this familiar place, you are dealing with homeostasis, as we talked about in the last chapter.

If you plan to work at getting new and better results, you are going to have to break through your comfort zone. Or at least make it much bigger. Don't worry too much, though, because this is exactly what you want to do in order to succeed. It's the process of growth and it's the way things happen; you've gone through it time and time again to get to where you are right now. Also, you are in good shape, since you are now in possession of techniques that are just what you need in order to get the job done.

Take heart in this: The most powerful element of the comfort zone is that it's unconscious. Most people don't even know it exists, and therefore never examine it. Just putting it under the microscope of your attention reduces much of its power. Also, remember that homeostasis starts out as your enemy when you are seeking change, but if you persist past the initial attempts, it then becomes your friend because it will support you in your new efforts. So stay the course. Again, it's a cycle that we've been going through all of our lives. It's nothing new.

What Will My Friends Think?

Often, the fear of how others will judge us can inhibit our efforts to improve. Something that frequently happens to students who haven't been successful in the past is that they are afraid to be seen working to be successful. They don't want to stand out from the crowd. A certain amount of this isn't hard to understand because of a natural desire among kids to fit in. But this can go too far and hurt your ability to become who you want to be. If you have friends that give you a hard time because you are working to be more successful, you might want to ask yourself some questions.

First of all, what do you think you will gain by being unsuccessful, especially if you have the capacity to do better? How are you going to benefit? It's true that there *are* benefits in such a situation (remember secondary gain?), but you have to decide for yourself whether they will outweigh the benefits you will receive from doing your best. It's your call.

Kids do make fun of other students, sure, but I've always noticed that when it comes down to it, they generally respect the students who do well (even as they rip on them). Regardless of what others say concerning your effort to improve, do you actually think they are going to respect you if you screw up? Why would they? If any one of them felt that they could do better themselves, do you think they wouldn't seek to do so?

Don't let others' reactions hold you back. Even if someone else gets on you for the changes you are making, don't worry too much. Just as it is an adjustment for you, it's also an adjustment for them. If you stick with it, they will get used to it as well. Besides, the positive feelings you receive from your new success will more than compensate for any initial discomfort you experience as you break out of your comfort zone.

> *Accept the challenges,*
> *so that you may feel the exhilaration of victory.*
> *—George S. Patton*

But What About My Excuses?

Another little comfort zone quirk about getting started on this stuff is best summed up in the statement, "If I do this, I won't have any more excuses for not succeeding." It's comfortable in your present state, even if this state is not allowing you to produce the results that you want. The fear comes in when you start to realize that access to this stuff *will* allow you to move toward your dreams and goals. It's one thing to be doing less than you want to, and not know why it's happening or not know how to do anything about it. It is quite another to *know* ways to get far greater results. Then, what possible excuse do you have for not achieving those results? This kind of thinking can put undue stress on you and stop you from getting started.

But it doesn't have to be this way. First of all, *any* degree of work in this direction will bring you some positive results. You get as much out of it as you put into it. Therefore, if you do any of this work, you aren't going to fail completely. Of course, there are always possibilities that you might fall down along the way, sometimes to the point of stopping altogether for a while. Maybe even a long while. But falling down is not failing unless you never get back up.

For many people, an excuse is better than an achievement
because an achievement, no matter how great,
leaves you having to prove yourself again in the future
but an excuse can last for life.
—*Eric Hoffer*

Coming Back After a Break

Maybe you've already had this happen to you and are just getting back to it after a break and are reading this chapter again, or are reading the whole book again in order to get help in starting over. Well, so what if you are starting over? You fall down, you get up. Congratulations for starting over. I won't bore you with how many times I had to start over, even with writing this book. Life is made up of a series of starting overs. It doesn't make any difference how many times it takes you to get it right because succeeding is a process, not a destination. The true progress that you get, the real benefit that comes from your doing this, is not what you get in the way of stuff, but what you *become* through your achievements.

It's like hard work. The greatest thing about working hard isn't the fruits it brings, (nice as they are) but in the way you feel, the state you are in while working. If you doubt this, look at all the successful people known for their work habits. Do they quit working after they become successful enough to live comfortably without any extra work? We often hear people say that they would retire and do nothing if they suddenly became successful, but the people who actually do become successful rarely just retire. They know that the process is the key, not the stuff it brings. And speaking of hard work, it is just the stuff that another one of our possible fears is made of.

Working Smarter, Not Harder

Are you worried that this is going to mean too much extra effort? If so, stop for a second. The truth is, it's not really a matter of working harder. It's more a matter of working smarter, of focusing more efficiently in order to get the results that you want. You are using the same amount of energy as before; the only difference is that you're aiming it all in the same direction instead of scattering it all over the place. It's the difference between a laser and a splatter.

Also, there's something called the *drag of resistance*. It's the amount of effort needed to resist something, to stop something from moving forward. Think of how hard you have to apply the brakes on your bike after cruising down a big hill, and how hot they get when you're done. By eliminating the drag of resistance that used to hold back your efforts in the past, you free up a tremendous amount of energy that can now be used toward your new goals. Ask anybody who is successfully involved in a project or endeavor and they will tell you that the more they get into it, the less tired they feel.

The more one works, the more willing one is to work.
—Lord Chesterfield

Nothing is easy to the unwilling.
—Thomas Fuller

The drag of resistance takes far more out of you than hard work does because it stops all momentum. When you are moving ahead willingly, you develop momentum and it takes far less energy to *keep* going than it takes to *get* going. Again, think of riding your bike. Doesn't it take much more effort to reach your maximum speed than it does to keep going at maximum speed once you achieve it? Once you get momentum, you have won half the battle. So don't worry that achieving far greater levels of success will require far greater effort than your less successful results required. It's about working smarter, not harder. It's also a matter of focus.

Think of a magnifying glass burning a hole in a piece of paper. It isn't using any more energy than was there before you started. The glass just focuses the sunlight, concentrating its power. When you line up your focus with your goals, you are doing the same thing—you are working with a laser instead of a splatter. It makes all the difference in the world.

If I Do It Once, I'll Always Have to Do It

Similarly, there's a frequently expressed objection along the lines of: "If I succeed, people will expect me to get results like this all the time, and I'll always have to work just as hard." This fear springs from what many students feel to be unrealistic expectations coming from parents and teachers. But this is in fact a case of having trouble with the comfort zone and not realizing who is *really* keeping score.

It's understandable that you might be concerned about the pressure of expectations. After all, it *is* going to be there. The problem is in the perception of where most of this pressure will be coming from. Think of it this way. Let's say that you worked at this stuff for a while and succeeded at getting A's for a quarter or semester. Do you really think that you are going to want to go back to getting C's, D's, or F's after all of the pleasure you received from getting the A's?

Believe me, I've been on both sides of this fence. I received horrible grades in high school and I've gotten straight A's in college. There was no pressure or expectation from *anyone* that could have had nearly as much influence on my behavior as succeeding in getting the A's did. I had no desire to get rotten grades again, and the drag of resistance it would have taken to fall back to that level would have been far more exhausting than anything I was putting out to maintain the A's.

Don't worry about other people's expectations. Success is a lot more fun than failure. Once you get a taste, you will be happy to maintain it, and your enthusiasm toward doing so will be more than enough to keep you going in the right direction.

Losing the Whole Because of a Part

Unless, of course, you self-sabotage. *Self-sabotage,* or undermining yourself, is an ugly idea, but it happens quite frequently as people begin to succeed. It goes back to the comfort zone. Many of us have learned to see ourselves belonging within certain limits, of deserving only so much because of actions other people have taken or things they have said about us. Haven't we all had the delightful experience when we were little (or maybe not so little), of some teacher, parent, or friend telling us that we were stupid, or lazy, or bad, or whatever, when they were angry with us? Because we believed them, their limited perceptions or beliefs about us became *our* limiting perceptions or beliefs. Now, once we begin to move away from these limits, it is quite possible that we might get uncomfortable and start behaving in ways that would ensure that we get back into our comfort zone.

Self-sabotage happens because some aspect of the results you want bothers you and your mind is trying to help you avoid it. The problem is that by avoiding the part, you lose out on the rest, on the aspects you do want.

Find Out Why the Sabotage Doesn't Make Sense

When examined, many of the reasons why we self-sabotage do not make a whole lot of sense. But when has *that* stopped us from doing anything? Luckily, once you see self-sabotage for what it is, it gets much easier to work it out and keep moving in the direction you want to go.

Fortunately, we've already touched on much of what goes into self-sabotage. For example, say you've gotten excited about the possibilities of working with this stuff. There you are raring to go, but you're afraid it is going to take too much effort. So you don't follow through, even though you really do want the results. Well, you now have a better idea of how succeeding means working smarter instead of harder, of using a laser instead a splatter. As you become more comfortable with this new idea (and yes, programming it in as a new belief is an excellent idea), the sabotage that may have been troubling you in the past will lose its grip and you won't have to fight it as much.

Similarly, another self-sabotage problem is that some people start succeeding and begin to feel uncomfortable with their success because they haven't done anything like it before. So they feel they don't deserve it. Even worse, they feel that this isn't *them*, that they are somehow faking it. They feel it's only a matter of time before other people will catch on and they will be seen as the fakes that they are. Therefore, in order to stop this process of getting caught, they pull the plug on their efforts and get back to where it's comfortable—in their comfort zone.

Again, you now have more insight into this little demon. First of all, your efforts as well as your results in the past have nothing to do with the present or future. If you change your strategies and your habits into ones that have proven successful for other people, you can get similar results, too. Who cares about what you could or couldn't do before?

Hey, when you were a baby you couldn't even stand up, right? If your identity changes, *you* change. Do you think you were faking it when you learned how to ride a bike? Believe me, you certainly didn't know how to do it before that first time. Do you remember your parents or any of your friends saying, "Hey, who do you think you are riding that bike like that? You can't *really* ride it. Get off that bike and go back to walking like you should be doing, you big fake!" As a matter of fact, if you were the first to successfully learn to ride, you can be sure that your friends wanted to be just like you. So what's different now?

If you haven't been successful in the past, it makes no difference whatsoever. You didn't know how to ride a bike, you learned to ride a bike. You didn't know how to be a successful student, you learn how to become a successful student. No one is going to think you are a fake or think that you don't deserve it. At least no one worth listening to. (Please know that when someone is getting down on someone else's success, 99% of the time the real reason is that they are trying to compensate for their own feelings of inadequacy.)

Weeding Out Self-Sabotage

So it goes with any form of self-sabotage. Once you have a handle on this stuff, it's much easier to deal with the issues that come up from time to time. First, find out what you are trying to avoid. Then, examine it to see why you might want to avoid it. (Remember secondary gain?) If you can spot an error in reasoning, this will begin to weaken the self-sabotaging tendency's power because it won't be able to go by unquestioned any longer. But this is only a beginning. You know by now that it doesn't make any difference if a disempowering belief makes sense or not. If it's programmed into your mind's computer, you are going to run it. What you do is recognize it so that you can begin changing the program. With all of your new information and tools, you can now do this much easier than you ever could before. *If* you get working on it.

Please Don't Start Trying Now

Now that you have a better understanding of how fears can keep you from getting going, this would seem to be the perfect time for me to encourage you to take this material and try hard to reach the goals you have set for yourself, wouldn't it? But I'm not going to do it. I am not going to tell you to *try*. It might sound strange, but if you try, you will probably *not* succeed. This is an important concept to grab hold of, and it is one that often meets resistance.

So often we are told to try. "Give it a try." "Try harder." "All you have to do is try." On the surface, these encouragements sound like good advice, since trying sounds like a positive thing to do. But "trying" contains built-in failure because deep in the subconscious, where the mind conducts the large part of its business, "try" means the same thing as "fail." Of course, this doesn't mean that try always means fail. Words have different meanings and usages for different situations, and your mind, being the sophisticated piece of work that it is, can tell the difference. Obviously, when you use the word *try* in any of its other meanings, such as trying a new recipe or trying out for a team or something, your mind isn't going to interpret it as failing. When I speak of trying in this context, however, I mean in the sense of attempting to accomplish something. These are the instances when it can easily become a code for failure.

Well, at Least I Failed

This idea sounds crazy at first, but think about it. When you get in a situation where you do not succeed, what's the first thing you say? "Well, at least I tried." And maybe you did. But listen closely to what is happening down where your programs are. If you fail at something and say that you tried, or you have someone telling you that it's ok because "at least you tried," it becomes an excuse for your failure. Whether it's a good excuse or a bad excuse doesn't matter. It's still an excuse, something designed to get you off the hook for failing. Now, if every time you fall short on a goal, or project, or assignment, or test, or whatever, you fall back on the excuse, "Well, at least I tried," then your mind links the two ideas together. Once this link is established (and it doesn't take long), every time you say, "I'll try," your mind hears "try" and, because of past experience, joins it with "fail." Therefore, when you say, "I'll try," you are sending your mind the subtle message that you don't expect to succeed, and your mind will accommodate you.

> *Do or do not. There is no try.*
> —*Yoda*

Take This Little Test

If you don't think this is true, put yourself to a little test. The next time you find yourself in a situation where you hear yourself say, "I'll try," stop and say, "I will *do* it," instead. If it feels like jelly in your belly, a feeling like you aren't *really* comfortable with the commitment, know that you have set yourself up to fall short. You might come close, but you probably won't make it the whole way.

What were you after when you first stated your intention? Did you really think you would succeed? If you did, then you wouldn't have any trouble saying, "I will *do* it," as opposed to, "I will *try*." If you do have trouble saying, "I will do it," then somewhere deep down, you don't feel like you will get the job done. On some level, there's a lack of confidence or some other block. That's all it takes. As you've learned by now, you are going to produce results consistent with your belief, and your belief is not as confident as you want it to be. "Try," no matter how close you come, means "fail."

Here's an example to prove my point: Jerry Rice scored more touchdowns than anyone in the history of the NFL. Of course, after every one of them, his teammates congratulated him in the end zone and on the sideline. In fact, you could say that Rice has probably been congratulated by more teammates than any other player in the league. So, in the thousands of times he's been congratulated, how many players do you think came up and said, "nice *try*, Jerry!"? That's right, zero. They saved that for the times he dropped the ball.

Remember, you have a great interest in being right, and your mind will guide you toward the result you believe you should get. Since your mind interprets "try" as "fail," your efforts will guide you in that direction. Even if you're not paying attention and are thinking you *might* succeed this time.

I'll Try to Call You

Another reason why "trying" leads to *not* succeeding is that we quite often use "I'll try" when we have no intention of doing something. You know how it works. Someone asks you to do something and you don't really want to, but you can't get out of it gracefully. What do you tell them? "Well, I'll *try*." "I'll try to get back to you on that." "I'll try to be there." "I'll try to be back by then." "I'll try to get in touch with her." "I'll try harder next time." Of course, you know that you're not really going to do it, even though you say you are going to try. Well, guess what? Your mind doesn't take you any more seriously when you say it to yourself than it does when you say it to someone else. It knows better. When you say, "I'll try," all it hears is, "I'm not really going to do it."

Don't Try to Do It—Expect to Do It

So what are you going to do? Are you at the mercy of the "I'll try" trap? Of course not. But if you've been accustomed to saying, "I'll try," or using, "at least I tried" as an excuse, then you will have to do some programming. The nice thing is that, by now, you already know how to do this. It shouldn't be that big of a deal. Here's what you do: From now on, get in the habit of saying, "I'll do it" instead of, "I'll try." Maybe it doesn't sound like that much of a difference, but it is. Do you think for a moment that when Barry Bonds goes up to the plate that he is *trying* to get a hit? No no no no no. Barry Bonds walks up to the plate with every intention of getting a hit. No matter how many times he doesn't come through, he *still* goes up there knowing that he is going to get a hit *this* time.

Of course, he is not alone. Just like Michael Jordan, Charles Barkley, one of the all-time NBA greats, always said that when the game was on the line and there was one last shot to be made, he *demanded* the ball. And he expected to make that shot *every single time*. Did he make every shot? Of course not. But it made no difference whatsoever to Sir Charles. When the time came, he *still* expected to make the shot, and that made all the difference. He knew that he was *the* go-to guy, and he knew that in the same last shot situation, many players in the NBA *don't* want the ball. Sure, they might *try* to make the shot if it came to that, but they don't really expect to make it, and they would rather have someone else take it.

Again, it's not just in sports that this stuff is exhibited. Successful people in all walks of life learn to focus on *doing* instead of trying to do. It's an attitude. A major difference between the successful person and the unsuccessful one is that the successful person goes into each new situation expecting to succeed right away, while the unsuccessful person generally feels that he or she will fail at first. Certainly, since I have already said that the successful person will often fail along the way to success, I am not implying that success is automatic just because it is expected. But the *expectation* of success goes a long way toward speeding up the process. And that's what this is all about, improving the odds of your succeeding.

If there are failures along the way, however, the successful person doesn't dwell on them. He or she just focuses on the positive elements, learns what there is to learn and moves on, expecting to succeed the next time. The unsuccessful person, on the other hand, will dwell on the failures, ignore the positive aspects of the situation, and assume that he or she is destined to fail, thereby giving up.

Every great work, every great accomplishment,
has been brought into manifestation through holding to the vision,
and often just before the big achievement,
comes apparent failure and discouragement.
—Florence Scovel Shinn

Knowledge Is Not Power

There's a well-known saying that knowledge is power. As good as it sounds, it *isn't* true. Many people have the knowledge and, sad to say, they haven't become any more successful. This is because merely *having* the knowledge is not enough. In fact, many of the students who read this book will not succeed. That's right, despite having access to the same information that so many diverse people throughout history have used successfully, they will *still* fail. The saddest part is that the reason they will fail has nothing to do with lack of talent, or lack of resources, or lack of opportunity. It will have nothing to do with the school they go to, the teachers they have, or anything on the outside.

They will fail because they will not *do* anything with the information that they have been given. They will not *receive* it. Imagine that. It's like wanting to get into a locked room and not using the key that has been given to you to open the door. It sounds insane that someone would not use these keys to success once they had access to them, but it's all too true.

> *Nothing will work unless you do.*
> —*John Wooden*

Every year, thousands of copies of books are sold that contain information similar to what I've presented here. Every year, thousands of people attend seminars, classes, and workshops (often at great expense) to learn this same information in one form or another. And sad to say, they never *do* anything with the knowledge they get at these events. Knowledge is *not* power. *Action*, based on that knowledge, is.

So, here at the end, we come back to the beginning. Now that you've finished this book, you have a greater understanding of the power in the elements of achievement. You also have some constructive ways of dealing with the junk that gets in the way of your using them in a positive manner. Like I said at the start, there are no tricks or gimmicks. There isn't any hocus-pocus magic wand. There's just you and your desire to excel far beyond anything you've done up to this point. With an understanding of how to use the elements of achievement, along with the will to do so, you don't need that other stuff, anyway.

Remember, whether we are talking about long-term or short-term goals, when it comes to consistently achieving success in anything, it all comes down to the achievement process: Know exactly what you are going for, consistently see yourself as having already accomplished it, fully expect that you will do so, and feel that way.

Will you be one of the many people who will wait until "someday" to put it to use, or will you be one of the ones who will begin today? Only you know. You've been given some very effective keys, but it is still up to *you* to unlock the door. Do it. Please, please, please, *do* it.

I will do this.

I *will* do this.

I will *do* this.

I will do *this.*

To know and not do is not yet to know.
—Zen proverb

Even if you are on the right track,
you'll get run over if you just sit there.
—Will Rogers

The great end of life is not knowledge, but action.
—Thomas Henry Huxley

Knowing is not enough; we must apply.
Willing is not enough; we must do.
—Johann Wolfgang Goethe

The world cares very little about what a man or woman knows;
it is what the man or woman is able to do that counts.
—Booker T. Washington

The future belongs to those
who believe in the beauty of their dreams.
—Eleanor Roosevelt

The world is round and the place which may seem like the end
may also be only the beginning.
—Ivy Baker Priest

About the Author

Fred Hageman has been on both sides of the academic divide in his own school experience. Throughout high school, he was a poor student with an admittedly awful attitude and barely graduated. After completely overhauling his approach, however, he went on to college and graduated with highest honors. He knows first-hand the challenges students face, as well as what is needed to overcome them.

Over the course of his career in education, Mr. Hageman has taught high school English, reading, Special Education, and English as a Second Language. He has extensive experience working with students of all ages, ability levels, and backgrounds. He has made teaching the elements of achievement his primary focus because he feels that this crucial component is being overlooked in the usual efforts to help students succeed.